'Jenny Gray has thought deeply about the way churches can work with schools, and has developed materials which can engage and excite teachers and young people alike . . . I warmly commend her work.'

The Rt Revd Paul Bayes, Bishop of Hertford

RE Active Church

Connecting every primary school child with the Christian story

Jenny Gray

First published in Great Britain in 2012

Society for Promoting Christian Knowledge
36 Causton Street
London SW1P 4ST
www.spckpublishing.co.uk

British Library Cataloguing-in-Publication Data
A catalogue record for this book is available from the British Library

ISBN 978-0-281-06766-4
eBook ISBN 978-0-281-06767-1

1 3 5 7 9 10 8 6 4 2

Typeset by Graphicraft Limited, Hong Kong
Printed in Great Britain by Ashford Colour Press

eBook by Graphicraft Limited, Hong Kong

Produced on paper from sustainable forests

Contents

Foreword

I am now the proud grandparent of four superb little children. I love them to bits and long for them to have the best things life has to give. So an underlying question that's always hanging around in my mind is, 'How will these little ones find faith?' Fortunately, they have wonderful, faith-full parents and that's clearly their best chance but, if they didn't have that good fortune, what then?

That's the dilemma the Church faces today, with fewer adults in each generation knowing the Christian story from the inside – or even from the outside. It's a story slipping out of a culture that's been fundamentally shaped by it. Christians believe that this is the world's defining story and one with which we need to engage if our restless hearts are ever to find their rest and fulfilment.

What we need, then, are imaginative ways of taking the Christian story into the hearts of our children so that they can engage with it, participate in it, wonder and puzzle over it and be moved by it. That is what Jenny Gray and her friends in Welwyn Garden City have done, in an innovative, creative but essentially simple way, which is now offered as a model to the wider Church.

This is a book packed with ideas and containing every detail any group could want if they are going to try and translate the model into other settings. Anyone with good sense and good faith could get involved and know that they are part of something truly worthwhile. I hope the ideas in this book will be used in hundreds of churches all over the land, as Christians reach out and find the risen Lord waiting for them in the schools that are shaping our children's future.

Then, perhaps, my question will be answered and our children will indeed find faith.

John Pritchard
Bishop of Oxford

Introduction
What is RE Active Church?

RE Active Church provides the format and resources for *any* church to invite Key Stage 2 children (Years 3 to 6, ages 7 to 11) from local primary schools, each term, to explore key RE themes of Christmas, Easter and the life and teaching of Jesus.

There is a four-year cycle of ready-to-use interactive material, with additional material for Key Stage 1 presentations in schools/visits to church, and adaptations for children with learning difficulties.

RE Active Church has been developed in a local church context by Christian teachers and extensively tried and tested over the last eight years. Although it has grown out of a particular church context, the format is designed to be easily replicable anywhere.

This book explains how to set up and run RE Active Church and provides all you need to run your own workshops. It provides material for a church to run one-hour workshops each term for primary school classes. Each one-hour workshop consists of a five-minute introduction to the whole class, four ten-minute activities in different parts of the church, and a fifteen-minute summing-up for the whole class. The children work in four small groups and move around the four activities to explore different aspects of the theme. You could begin with one workshop a year, at Christmas, for example, for just one class, or invite each class in the primary school every term.

The material is low-tech and low-cost – your most important resource will be people. RE Active Church does need a team of five helpers, but we explain how to recruit, train and get the best out of them (see Chapter 3).

How did RE Active Church begin?

In 1999, the St Francis of Assisi Church, Welwyn Garden City, held a Christmas Tree Festival. Some 50 groups, including local schools, decorated Christmas trees, and 2,000 people visited the church. The festival was a great fundraiser and an opportunity to reach out to the local community, so it became an annual event. The church recruited welcomers, put on special services and set up all-age reflective prayer stations, but we longed to do more to share the meaning of Christmas and encourage lots of people to visit the church, especially the children.

In 2003, a small team prepared the first RE Active Church workshops for our nearest primary school. We invited each class to come to church for an hour at a time to see the trees and find out more about Christmas, and 300 children came over 3 days! We explored the Christmas story and its meaning through small-group activities, excited by the huge privilege and responsibility of contributing to the education of generally un-churched children who would not otherwise come to the church.

The simple format of one class, one hour, one workshop with multisensory, interactive, small groups worked well. Feedback was positive from the school, our team of helpers, the vicar and congregation, so we did it again in 2004, with new material, and also invited the children from the local school for children with learning difficulties to share the experience (see Chapter 11).

Going beyond Christmas

Building on the positive response to our Christmas workshops, we decided to run something at Easter. So we invited the children again in spring 2005 to explore Holy Week and build on the relationships we had established at Christmas. Would our local primary school be interested in Easter, we wondered? The answer was 'yes' because Easter, like Christmas, is on the RE curriculum for each year of Key Stage 2 (both the story and its meaning for Christians). Hence Easter and Christmas workshops became part of our church and school events calendars.

What about the summer?

We decided to offer RE Active Church workshops in the summer, using the same format, to focus on the life and teaching of Jesus. That way, there would be a workshop each term, the summer one filling in the story between Jesus' birth at Christmas and his death and resurrection at Easter. This would also help teachers to cover the parts of the RE curriculum that relate to Jesus' life and questions of faith. So since 2005, the St Francis of Assisi Church has been providing RE Active Church workshops each term for the primary school in our parish and for two schools in neighbouring parishes as their headteachers heard what we were doing and asked to come too. We now see some 450 children over 4 or 5 days, 3 times a year.

What next?

In 2010 we started Messy Church,[1] a once-a-month, after-school session for children under the age of eleven and their carers to explore the Christian story through craft, worship and a shared meal. Like many churches, our team of volunteers followed the tried-and-tested format and materials of Messy Church with great success. Then a penny dropped! RE Active Church also has an easily replicable tried-and-tested format and we had made the resources, all of which could be used by other churches with their local schools if they were made available, so we started the process that has led to the publication of this book!

Who is behind RE Active Church?

The 'we' who began RE Active Church are, first and foremost, mums who know, from our own families,

the difficulty of bringing children to church on Sundays when there is sport to be played, fathers and friends don't go and church is not seen as 'cool'.

Since the 1980s, we have worked and prayed together as Sunday-school teachers, run holiday clubs and led child-friendly Sunday and midweek services. Since the 1990s, we have anguished over the decreasing numbers of children and young families at our church services – a trend that has accelerated since the millennium.

Like many churches, the St Francis of Assisi Church has a thriving Messy Church, Toddler Group, Rock Solid youth club, and linked Beaver, Cub, Scout and Rainbow groups, yet little apparent interest among the majority of children and parents in deepening a connection with the Christian faith and Sunday worship.

Carolyn Annand, Wendy Sellers and I trained as teachers and are used to preparing material for children and finding appropriate ways to engage with them. Sue Stilwell brings different skills from her background in human resources and work with the Scripture Union. We are an all-female team, but we have sought input from male youth workers who have been part of the ministry team. We were aware of the need to make provision for boys in our activities and to offer boys good role models.

We are on challenging faith journeys. Sue and I followed a call to the priesthood, Carolyn and Wendy to the lay reader ministry, but we share Christ's commission to all believers to go and tell others (Matthew 28.18-20), to pass on to others what Jesus has taught us about living in God's way, in God's world, with God's help.

We long for people to know about God, to recognize his presence in their lives and experience his love for themselves.[2] We hope that these resources will help you to do this for your local primary school children.

Summary: What's distinctive about RE Active Church?

Who is it for?

The RE Active Church format and material is suitable for any church to engage with any primary school. It is not limited to Anglican churches with established links to Church of England schools. The material can be adjusted to provide a different theological emphasis in its questions and its plenary sessions.

What does it provide?

- RE Active Church provides one-hour workshops in church for primary school classes. You could offer a workshop to just one class or to each class in a school (or schools). The four classes of a single-form entry school fit into one day at church. Whether you offer a single workshop or many, flexibility, prayer and patience is needed from both church and school(s) to timetable sessions.

- Depending on a church's size and resources, RE Active Church can be run in a single church, collaboratively across parishes or ecumenically, according to local circumstances. Relationships with schools are easy to maintain and nurture once the initial link between school and church has been made (more on page 15).

What does it cost?

RE Active Church material does not cost very much at all – an important consideration for most churches considering a new community venture.

Do we need lots of equipment?

RE Active Church material is low-tech. It can be adapted to include PowerPoint presentations and film clips, but its wide variety of resources means it can be run successfully in churches with minimal technology (see Chapter 4).

What about helpers?

RE Active Church helpers only work with ten minutes of material, which they repeat for each of the four small groups in a class, with increasing confidence and satisfaction. All the resources are set out clearly. You don't have to be a trained teacher or theologian to help with RE Active Church, so volunteers won't be scared to help (see Chapter 3)!

What difference can it make?

RE Active Church can be used to invite all primary school children in Years 3 to 6 to church for one hour at a time, three times a year, twelve times in a child's primary school career. Over the course of the four-year cycle of material, children can become increasingly familiar with the key stories of Christmas, Easter and the life and teachings of Jesus and their meaning for Christians today.

How do the children learn?

- Small-group activities allow children to ask questions, listen to each other as well as to adults, and respond to a range of materials. Active participation by each child is encouraged, but never forced. Blocks of activities, with movement from one to another, hold the children's attention.

- Extension work and open questions provide differentiated learning to accommodate different ages and abilities.

- Multisensory material and time for silent reflection introduce variety and cater for different learning styles. Some activities are verbal, some creative or arty, some physical.

- A simple craft activity, built up in each small group, is part of the children's learning experience and a means of reinforcing learning and connecting the experience in church with the children's homes.

- A simple take-away gift related to the workshop's theme is part of the welcome and learning experience.

- Provision is made for the needs of boys[3] through competition, challenge, trust and encouragement to help others, while also allowing boys to be reflective, less active and less competitive.[4]

- All children are encouraged to explore open-ended questions where there may be no 'right answer', something girls often find more difficult than boys.[5]

- Workshops create displays to be left in church to inform and involve the wider congregation.

- An optional song reinforces learning and capitalizes on children's love of rhythm and repetition.

The shape of this book

Part 1 explains the theory and background to RE Active Church and includes all the information you need to set up and run the workshops in your own church.

Part 2 includes all the workshop material, plus photocopiable summaries, handouts and craft templates. It also has extra material for a Key Stage 1 visit to church and an adaptation for a visit by children with learning difficulties, plus Christmas and Easter presentations for nursery or reception classes.

Part 1

RE Active Church practicalities

1
Working with schools

Why work with schools?

Mission has always been fundamental to who we are and what we do as church. The continued overall decline in average weekly attendance, however, has given the Church new challenges.

Many people in the UK today have little connection with the Church or real knowledge of the Christian story. In 2007, a British Sociological Association survey found that 45.7 per cent of the adult population had 'no religion', while Tearfund (April 2007) listed 33 per cent as 'unchurched', 33 per cent as 'dechurched', 15 per cent as attending church at least once a month and 10 per cent occasionally. Church clergy and congregations are ageing and attendance is forecast to fall by 55 per cent of the level in 1980 by 2020.[1]

In some sectors, there is outright hostility to the Church and religion of any kind. Religion is often misunderstood and equated with fundamentalism, terrorism, war, intolerance, outdated superstition or a preoccupation with sex. Media reports focus on the scandalous, while faith at its best is given little attention. Clergy in TV soaps and films are often figures of fun rather than people to look up to.

For many children, Christianity is no longer part of home life. Parents may have little understanding of Christian belief and practice, and if they don't go to church, their children are unlikely to think of going. If children have never been to church they don't know what it is like. Nationally just 4 per cent of children attended Sunday school in 2001.[2] Many predict this figure will drop to 1 per cent in 2020, although some dioceses do report increases in children attending worship.[3]

The challenge for churches

Many in the Church are recognizing this challenge and doing something about it. Some have started 'fresh expressions' of church. In addition, Mission Action Planning was developed in the London diocese in the 1990s to encourage parishes to agree a vision statement, engage in a mission audit and produce a clear Mission Action Plan (MAP).[4] Such plans include organizing work with children. This was 'warmly endorsed' for use in parishes by the Archbishops' Council and House of Bishops in May 2011[5] and has been commended in at least 20 dioceses and in denominations other than the Church of England.

Teaching children about God through word and practice is central to the Old Testament (Deuteronomy 6, 11.19) and part of the Great Commission Jesus gives his followers (Matthew 28.18-20). The Gospels (Matthew 19.13-14; Mark 10.13-16; Luke 18.15-20) show the importance of children to Jesus - his message is not reserved for grown-ups! The Church has a long history of contributing to religious and general education, but in today's sceptical, postmodern, secular culture, it is looking for new ways to connect with children who have little understanding or experience of the Christian faith. In the 2011 Anglican General Synod debate on education, the Archbishop of Canterbury Rowan Williams encouraged 'a critical partnership with the State that seeks to keep open for as many children as possible the fullest range imaginable of educational enrichment', assuming 'an honest and thoughtful exposure to the Christian faith'.[6]

Despite some positive initiatives by local churches, however, inviting children to church or church activities may not be enough. There are now many competing attractions on a Sunday. Our secular, postmodern society no longer treats Sunday as special and different. Even in Christian families, going to church has to compete with sport, shopping and other leisure activities.

A 2001 survey showed that 57 per cent of children who used to go to church stop before they leave primary school - the key age for stopping being between seven and ten years of age.[7] RE Active Church provides a small but regular and positive contact with church, which can contribute to children making up their own minds about the Christian faith.

Children's experiences of church

Children's experience of church is varied, but for those who currently go to church or who once went and have now stopped, it is not always positive, despite genuine attempts by churches to welcome children:

- Sunday congregations may be largely middle-aged or elderly – two churches in five in England have no children or youth work;[8]

- it can be difficult to engage with church music and liturgy – even all-age services can seem an alien world that children do not understand;

- men are under-represented in children's work in churches, which means a shortage of positive role models for boys;

- children's groups may lack critical mass – primary school age children, like teenagers, enjoy meeting and interacting with their peers;

- more churches now employ children's workers, but their work is often under-resourced and priority given to adults in the congregation.

Peter Brierley's survey in 2001[9] of ten-year-olds lists the top five reasons children give for not going to church as:

1 it's boring;

2 isn't cool;

3 can't be bothered;

4 other things to do;

5 friends don't go.

Also significant were:

- no parental encouragement;

- don't get up early;

- it's irrelevant;

- feel out of place.

The survey highlights the importance of churches taking the initiative, investing time and resources to work with schools, welcome children to church and present the Christian faith in authentic, creative and enjoyable ways that change these views.

The advantage of running RE Active Church workshops is that they engage children in their existing class friendship groups through creative and age-appropriate material. They also go against the stereotype that no one laughs in church!

Will schools be open to an approach from the local church?

Anecdotal evidence suggests that primary schools are currently receptive to approaches from churches, and churches are eager to work with children.[10] There is growing interest in the partnership between churches and schools beyond the traditional religious assembly, and there are some excellent initiatives, such as RE Inspired,[11] Stream Sacred Spaces,[12] the Diocese of Gloucester's resources for festivals[13] and 'Easter Cracked' and 'Christmas Unwrapped' presentations for Year 6 children.[14]

How RE Active Church can help schools

There are a number of reasons for schools to be positive about an approach from a local church, one of which is that it could help them meet the requirements of the RE curriculum. Although it is not a statutory part of the National Curriculum, RE remains a compulsory subject in schools and, at present, the teaching of RE is governed by the locally agreed syllabus. All children are required to learn about and learn from religions and their beliefs in RE. RE seeks not only to impart knowledge but also to develop understanding of religious experiences, feelings and attitudes. RE is also expected to contribute to the spiritual, moral, social and cultural development of pupils.

- RE Active Church supports teachers, some of whom may have little experience of church, prayer or worship, in meeting the requirements of the RE curriculum to teach key elements of Christianity and its meaning for Christians.

- Schools are also required to visit local places of worship. Visits, including visits to churches, enhance pupils' educational experience and help them connect with their local community and cultural heritage.

- RE Active Church is cross-curricular, helping schools cover aspects of RE in imaginative and enjoyable ways that spill over into other subjects, including PSHE, art, music, geography, history and technology.

One teacher's follow-up work with her class included designing and producing four acetate 'stained-glass' window panels for the church, to the delight of members of the congregation and the children on subsequent visits. The RE Active Church workshop 'ticked boxes' for the art and technology as well as RE syllabuses.

- RE Active Church resources take account of different learning styles, ages and abilities of children in school Years 3–6. Material for each workshop should be sent to the RE coordinator in each school ahead of visits to church. Feedback should be invited from schools before and after visits.

Other benefits

The resources help to teach values. Children's role models are often footballers, music, TV and film celebrities who are glamorous, rich and famous, but not necessarily happy or healthy, and who don't always behave responsibly!

The government-commissioned review, 'Letting children be children', by Reg Bailey, chief executive of the Mothers' Union,[15] highlights widespread concern over the sexualization and commercialization of childhood. This follows academic studies by Professor Tanya Byron in 2008[16] on the impact of new technology on children, Professor David Buckingham in 2009[17] on the commercialization of children and Dr Linda Papadopoulos in 2010[18] on the sexualization of young people. In partnership with schools, RE Active Church challenges the prevailing consumer-driven, materialistic, 'me first', celebrity culture and reinforces values taught across the curriculum. We encourage all children to:

- be open to new ideas, people and situations, be willing to question;
- establish priorities – to think about what is important in their lives and in the world;
- value themselves as individuals with unique and different gifts;
- do their best and value their best as good enough;
- respect other people as unique and gifted in different ways;
- be aware of other people's needs, be kind, generous, patient and able to exert self-control;
- be aware that actions have consequences and take responsibility for their actions;

- admit when they are wrong and act accordingly;
- be willing to contribute to the life of the community and realize that they can make a difference, however small;
- do what they can to care for the environment;
- learn to express ideas and emotions;
- be willing to ask for and give help;
- persevere.

Implicit in these values, which churches foster in their work with schools, is the 'fruit of the Spirit [is] love, joy, peace, patience, kindness, generosity, faithfulness, gentleness, and self-control' (Galatians 5.22–23, NRSV). *The Message*, which puts the text of the Bible in contemporary language, phrases this same passage as follows: 'affection for others, exuberance about life, serenity . . . a willingness to stick with things . . . compassion . . . loyal commitments, not needing to force our way in life, able to marshal and direct our energies wisely'.

Does RE Active Church aim to convert children?

RE Active Church does not aim to convert children, but rather to assist primary school(s) with an area that many teachers find daunting, lending them the Church's personal understanding and experience. Thus, RE Active Church aims to help children learn about the Christian faith as part of their history and culture from people for whom it has meaning. In fact, making a contribution to the education of large numbers of unchurched children is a great privilege and huge responsibility for Christians that must not be abused – a school is not a pond to fish in!

RE Active Church aims to equip children to make their own informed choices about religious faith and practice. It is never appropriate to use these workshops to impose faith on them. Indeed, this is made clear to both RE Active Church helpers and the schools taking part in workshops in the handouts provided (see Chapter 9).

The RE Active Church workshops are not a guaranteed way of getting children to church on Sundays, but are instead an opportunity for regular Christian input into primary school life. Like the sower in Jesus' parable (Mark 4.1–20), RE Active Church scatters seeds of welcome and engages children with the Christian story. Others may reap where we sow, as Paul reminds the church in Corinth (1 Corinthians 3.5-9).

> *One mum with no previous church connection currently comes to our midweek pram service because, some 20 years ago, 'a nice vicar' used to take her school assemblies on Friday mornings!*

The workshops therefore build on regular weekly contact with local children in school assemblies/ collective worship, and support and encourage Christian children, who are often in a minority in schools.

Is it appropriate for children of other faiths?

Some 6 per cent of the UK population belong to other faiths.[19] RE Active Church does not undermine children of other faiths because the RE curriculum in schools introduces every child to the key elements of the Christian faith. Religious differences need to be acknowledged as part of developing mutual respect, and inclusion is central to the ethos of schools.

Schools must obtain parental consent for church visits and, just as for religious assemblies, parents may withhold permission for their children to take part in RE Active Church. To date, this has not happened in our experience.

Making links with the wider community

RE Active Church helps the local church to serve the wider community, not just schools. The workshops

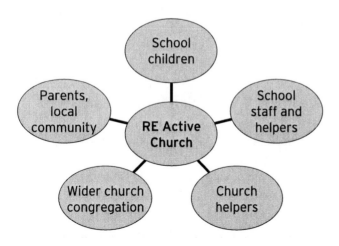

Figure 1 RE Active Church and the wider community

are a visible sign of God's generous, loving care for all people. Visits to church impact not only the children and teachers who take part but also the church helpers and, through both these groups, the wider congregation and community.

Links with schoolchildren, teachers and parents may be built on over time by taking religious assemblies in schools, supporting school events such as plays, fêtes and carol services, offering general help, such as hearing children read, helping them cook or garden, and extending invitations to special services and events at church.

Supporting the school community

RE Active Church fosters a caring relationship with school staff and helpers, who join in workshops alongside the children or talk to an RE Active Church helper over a coffee. It's an opportunity for people who may not normally come to church to share personal or school news of children, births, marriages, deaths and difficulties. Care continues in the staffroom, office and playground when we visit schools for religious assemblies - an informal and valued chaplaincy!

Our church also offers to pray for particular school needs, and includes local schools in the parish intercessions at the start of term, exam time and when Ofsted inspections are due, as well as Education Sunday and RE Active Church visits.[20] This is a great way of supporting and affirming school staff in their demanding work.

Working with other school years

RE Active Church provides resources for primary school pupils at Key Stage 2 (Years 3-6), but requests are regularly made for Year 2 classes to visit our church as part of their RE curriculum, so material for a Key Stage 1 visit is included in Chapter 11.

In addition to regular weekly primary school religious assemblies, we have also been asked to provide Christmas and Easter presentations for the local nursery and reception classes in schools, so Key Stage 1 material for these is also included in Chapter 11. Other local schools also ask to come to church with other year groups for their carol services and Christmas concerts and invite us to their harvest celebrations, so it is important to be adaptable.

What about secondary schools?

The need to work with children in secondary schools is undeniably great. The decision to omit RE from the 2010 list of English Baccalaureate subjects means that the future of RE in secondary schools – apart from faith schools – is uncertain, although it remains compulsory until the age of 16.

The transition from primary to secondary education involves major changes in children's friendship groups, activities and physiology, which tend to have a negative impact on their attendance at church. Quoting the Rakes survey 2001, Peter Brierley suggests 'a year or two into secondary school . . . they leave – in droves. Perhaps three-quarters of twelve-year-olds in church will leave in their next two years.'[21]

Working with secondary schools carries practical difficulties too, as the large number of pupils and staff makes organizing visits to church considerably more complicated than for primary schools. It is also more difficult to recruit helpers from the congregation to work with teenagers and older children than for events with Key Stage 2 children.

RE Active Church chooses to focus on building a strong foundation with each child in primary school over a four-year period. Statistics 'show the importance of having good teaching for those aged seven to ten years of age. These years lay the foundation for a child's long-term reaction to church (and maybe Christianity).'[22]

We work in different ways with our local secondary school, however, including workshops for Year 8 classes to explore baptism in church, taking occasional lessons in school using the Step[23] project material and sharing in an ecumenical lunchtime drop-in club. The church also runs a School Refusers' Group on Monday mornings for a small number of pupils who have real difficulty adjusting to secondary school – church is a safe place to improve their social skills and communication.

The benefits

We have found that, far from being hostile, local schools have welcomed what we have to offer. Here are some comments from teachers:

RE Active Church workshops help children realize they all belong to a bigger family. RE Active Church may not be in line with their own belief and practice, but it is something that will broaden each child's holistic education. My staff have benefited hugely from working alongside the church . . . different approaches, different faces, different voices sharing and reinforcing the same message.

Vicky Parsey, Headteacher, Applecroft School

We are always looking for ways of enabling our children to be included in their wider community and our regular work with the church is a big part of being able to do that. One facet of this link is our ability to enable our children to be givers rather than receivers, for example in our harvest giving to the church-run Food Bank.

Judith Chamberlain, Headteacher, Lakeside School (a school for children with severe learning difficulties)

Going to St Francis Church has allowed the children to learn in an environment other than the classroom. Members of the local community have brought learning alive and enthused the children to investigate further the different topics covered. The activities have been planned in a way that allows all children to take part and challenges their ideas on the various topics. The children have enjoyed coming, as have the staff, and are slowly discovering the community they are part of.

Angharad Morris, Headteacher, Templewood School

Thoroughly enjoyable activities that have become a welcome tradition within our school. 'Hands on' experience that can then be applied within the classroom. **Teachers from Peartree School**

The children said:

When I go to church I enjoy learning new stuff about Jesus. Going to church is learning but in a fun way. **Ana**

What I like about church is the peace and quiet and working in groups. The people there are nice and they explain the story of Easter and Christmas and give you a chocolate. **Harrison**

They make it really fun to learn about Christianity by acting it out or doing an activity. Once I got to be Jesus. **Tim**

One of the messages I've picked up is that you should try to forgive. **Matthew**

I like walking to and from church with my friends. You get time to discuss all the activities. **Daisy**

Questions to think through

- How many primary schools are within walking distance of your church?
- What links does your church already have with local primary school(s)? How could you build on this?
- Jesus stresses the importance of children in God's kingdom - how great a priority does your church place on working with all the children in the locality or parish?

2

How RE Active Church works

RE Active Church takes place in church

Not every primary school is near a church. Our three primary schools have a 15- to 20-minute walk to our church. We *could* run our workshops in the schools, but we believe that coming to church is really important, for several reasons.

- Church is the best place to explore the Christian story because the signs and symbols of faith are all around. There is much to see in church that sparks questions and wonder. All churches, whatever their age and other uses, are holy, set apart for prayer and the worship of God.

- It could be the first time children have crossed the threshold of a church. In RE Active Church an unfamiliar and possibly frightening building becomes a known place of welcome. What had been a place for others becomes their place too – a place where they can feel at home, as well as a place for wonder.

- Coming into a church as children can facilitate future contacts later in their lives. Many adults come to church for 'hatching, matching and dispatching' (that is, baptisms, weddings and funerals), harvest festivals, carol services or Christingle services.

- The old mission order of 'believe, behave, belong' has been superseded by a new model of 'belong, believe, behave'. Children I meet who have no contact with church outside of school visits often say things like, 'This is my church' or 'I go to your church'.

- The obvious care lavished on the church building, together with the time and energy given by RE Active Church helpers in preparing and delivering workshops, convey positive messages – that our Christian faith matters and children are important to us and to God; they are worth time and effort.

In the parable of the wedding feast, Jesus says, 'Go . . . into the main streets, and invite everyone you find to the wedding banquet' (Matthew 22.9, NRSV). I believe that this includes inviting all primary school children to church!

RE Active Church promotes active learning

RE Active Church uses multisensory materials to engage children with different learning styles in active learning. We encourage participation through pictures, simple plays, quizzes, acted stories, visual aids and artefacts, music, song, reflective silence and craft. We invite, but never force, a response.
RE Active Church:

- offers opportunities for wonder, creativity and fun that reflect both the transcendence (otherness) and immanence (closeness) of God and helps children explore questions of meaning as, hopefully, part of a life-long journey;

- provides a safe place for children to ask questions, express ideas and feelings, doubts, hopes and fears, to be listened to and listen to others;

- provides differentiated learning to accommodate the wide range of children in school Years 3-6 by using open questions and extension work;

- uses accessible, age-appropriate language and clarifies 'churchy' words to help children gain the vocabulary and confidence to talk about what they believe;

- values process over product – the craft projects do not have to be perfect and the helpers are encouraged to be flexible in their use of the materials – it does not matter if they do not cover everything providing they deal with the main points;
- gives a positive welcome and affirms the contribution of each child, reflecting God's unconditional acceptance and delight in every human being.

Taking it further

An hour in RE Active Church goes quickly! We often wish we had more time with each class and look for ways to follow up questions that arise after their visit. So, for example, we might offer an RE post box in the school(s), where children can leave notes with thoughts or questions that could be followed up in weekly assembly or other visits to church.

RE Active Church works in small groups

Jesus taught his disciples in small groups as well as speaking to crowds. Though twelve is too many for RE Active Church, groups of seven to eight children work well – small enough for each child to contribute, large enough to generate a range of ideas.

Working in small groups helps to build relationships between the children and helpers. Helpers can affirm and encourage each child in their contributions to discussions and help them listen to one another as they explore the Christian stories and their meanings. The small group offers space for each child to express ideas and ask questions, although no one is forced to speak. We ask the teachers to put the children into four groups before they come to church – they know which children work well together and which are best kept apart.

RE Active Church has an easy-to-follow structure

Each one-hour workshop is divided into six parts:

- a five-minute introduction to the whole class
- four ten-minute small group activities in different parts of the church
- a 15-minute plenary conclusion for the whole class.

The helpers stay in the same place, in charge of one activity, which they repeat for the four small groups in each class. They work with just ten minutes of material, which means it's not too daunting for volunteers.

Our experience

In Welwyn Garden City, we run workshops that each last a day once a term. On each of those days, four classes come – two in the morning and two in the afternoon – with a lunch break that fits in with the school's timetable.

We have three local schools; they bring a total of 16 classes and we try to run all the sessions in a week. We work around times when the church is being used for other things and leave as many of the resources as possible in each of the areas where the small groups work. This keeps setting up and packing away to a minimum. You might decide, however, to run just a single workshop for a single class or keep workshops to either mornings or afternoons depending on when your church premises are being used.

Some helpers stay all day, others offer to come for just the mornings or just the afternoons. We give helpers the opportunity to change small groups, but most choose to stay with the material they are familiar with, growing in confidence with it as a result.

Recruiting, training and retaining helpers is a crucial part of the success of RE Active Church. See the next chapter for more on how to go about this.

3

Getting RE Active Church started

Persuading your church

Before doing anything else, it is really important to have and retain the support and interest of the whole congregation, beginning with the vicar or minister or ministry team. Approaches in each church will vary, but the opportunity offered in RE Active Church to engage whole classes of primary school children with the Christian story should convince churches with declining numbers of children, as well as churches with flourishing children's work who cannot reach every child in a local school, that this is worth doing.

A good plan of action is to arrange to talk with the vicar or minister or ministry team about the concept and perceived benefits of RE Active Church and provide them with a short summary – you could photocopy the beginning of the Introduction on page 1, along with the Summary box at the end, on pages 2–3. This could then be presented to the PCC and, once adopted, publicized to the wider church through sermons, magazine articles, talks to other groups and the church's website (if available).

RE Active Church needs only a small budget, but agreement has to be reached on which church resources can be used. In our case, we regularly share resources with our Youth and Children's Church. The LEA or local charities can be approached to cover the resources, such as posters and puppets.

A team of helpers is needed to plan and run each workshop. Volunteers need relevant checks, training and prayer support (see below).

Approaching and working with schools

RE Active Church can be a way of extending existing links with local primary schools, such as school assemblies or other collective worship, or making a new connection. Think through your existing links with schools – you may have a teacher, support staff, school governor or parent in your ministry team or in your congregation who could support you in introducing the concept of RE Active Church to a headteacher. You could then make an appointment to meet with the headteacher or RE coordinator to explore what your church can offer and what the school needs, and provide them with a written summary, either the one used to approach the church (see first point at the beginning of this chapter) and/or the handout Notes for schools included in Chapter 9. The headteacher or RE coordinator could also be shown a sample of the RE Active Church material and a one-hour workshop for one class could be offered as a 'taster' session. In our church, feedback on the material is solicited from schools both before and after workshops.

Agreeing RE Active Church dates with a primary school or schools can be a lengthy process because teachers are very busy people. I meet with the RE coordinator of our nearest primary school at the start of each term to look at dates, which then have to be agreed by all the staff. Once these dates have been put on the calendar, I repeat the process with the other schools. It takes patience, persistence, flexibility and prayer, but the opportunity to engage with all the local primary school children is well worth the effort. After half-term, I agree with each school the precise times of the workshops and the class numbers, then draw up a rota of church helpers (a sample rota is included in Chapter 9).

The RE Active Church organizer and team members may want to nurture regular contact with the schools, between termly workshops, by taking religious assemblies, supporting school events, such as plays, fêtes and carol services, and offering general help to, for example, hear children read, help them cook or garden or run or assist with lunchtime or after-school sports and other clubs. One primary school invites me to their Christmas pantomime trips and school plays and enlists me to judge their Comic Relief talent show. Indeed, relationships built in RE Active Church have opened the door to religious slots in school harvest festivals, jointly supporting charities such as Samaritan's Purse or the local food bank, partnership in the children's centre, being a community school governor and advertising church events such as Messy Church in the school newsletter.

Keeping your church informed

It is a good idea to provide regular reports for the vicar, minister or ministry team and PCC. The congregation can be updated too, via the church's website, parish magazine and weekly newsletter.

You may want to put on displays about the RE Active Church activities held, showing some of the work produced in the workshops, such as the net filled with named fish from the 'Who is Jesus?' workshop or the trellis prayer cross from 'Easter friends'. Ideas for such displays in your church are included in each workshop.

The whole congregation can be asked to pray for local schools at the start of each term, on Education Sunday, during Ofsted inspections and at exam times, as well as for each RE Active Church workshop.

The whole congregation can contribute in practical ways too - cutting out items for craft activities, such as 450 Easter egg cards or 900 small squares of silver foil! Others may like to donate resources or money for the workshops - providing some sweets for the children to take home, for example.

Recruiting a team

To run RE Active Church workshops you will need a team of five people, to include the following.

1 An organizer to:
   - coordinate arrangements between church and school;
   - arrange a rota of helpers;
   - keep a contact folder with details of helpers in case unforeseen events necessitate last-minute changes to the RE Active Church team;

   - enlist prayer support for the workshops and schools;
   - ensure helpers have the notes they need before the workshops;
   - provide any training that is needed;
   - check that everything necessary for the workshops is available;
   - thank helpers individually after workshops;
   - involve the wider congregation in publicizing and celebrating this work via the church's website, newsletter, magazine, PCC and APCM annual meeting.

If possible, the organizer should act as an extra person for the first workshop to check that each small group is running smoothly and 'troubleshoot' where needed. The organizer does not always have to be present, however, for example if more than one workshop is being offered in a day, and he or she may choose to be a helper for one of the small groups.

It is important to note that the organizer does not have to be a member of the ministry team, though it is useful to have members of both the laity and clergy engaged in building up relationships with schools, training and supporting helpers and involving the wider congregation through prayer and encouragement to volunteer as helpers.

The organizer needs to be enthusiastic about RE Active Church and able to enthuse others, so key qualities are being a good communicator, a people person, someone who is efficient and willing and able to delegate. If required, the role of organizer could be shared by two or more people.

2 Altogether, five helpers per session:
   - four to work with small groups;
   - one to be an extra pair of hands or 'runner' who troubleshoots, keeps time, moves groups on to the next activity, makes welcome teas and coffees for helpers and teachers and assists groups where needed, such as by filling jugs of water for the wedding at Cana activity.

Ideally, the organizer should be the extra person for the first workshop, to check that each small group is running smoothly and provide support as needed. After that, the extra person can be any helper. It may be someone who prefers a 'backroom job' rather than working directly with the children. It can be a way of introducing potential helpers to the team, allowing them to experience RE Active Church to see if it's for them. When there are several workshops in a day, being the extra person is a way of giving helpers a break, inasmuch as a change is as good as a rest!

3 The leader's role is:

- to welcome the groups to each session;

- to lead the introduction and plenary sessions;

- to conclude each workshop.

This can be any of the five helpers, but the role needs to be allocated in advance, so that the leader has sufficient time to become familiar with the material.

Helpers make or break RE Active Church

They say that faith is more caught than taught. The way Christians live out their faith often has a greater impact than anything we say, which is why Francis of Assisi, it is believed, told his followers to 'Preach the gospel everywhere. Use words if you have to.'

Recruiting and retaining the right team of helpers, therefore, is one of the most crucial tasks. It is more important to recruit people with the right qualities than to focus on professional training or expertise. Training can always be given prior to the workshops.

What qualities should RE Active Church helpers have?

RE Active Church helpers need to have enthusiasm and:

- a positive attitude to children, reflecting God's delight in every individual;

- a good rapport with children, the ability to engage and hold their attention;

- a commitment to the aims and remit of RE Active Church (outlined in Notes for RE Active Church helpers, Chapter 9);

- the ability and willingness to familiarize themselves with the material for their small group;

- flexibility in using the material, sensing when to move on in an activity or discussion;

- basic group management skills to encourage, but not force, everyone to participate and facilitate children listening to each other – allowing only one child to speak at a time;[1]

- an ability to listen carefully to children's questions and answers and affirm each contribution;

- confidence in responding simply to children's questions and answers, giving helpful responses such as, 'mmm', 'that's interesting', 'I wonder what others think', 'that sounds difficult/good', 'I don't know, but I'll try to find out for you later', 'Christians don't have all the answers', 'lots of Christians struggle with this';

- a willingness to talk naturally and simply about their own faith experiences when appropriate, without putting any pressure on children to share their beliefs;

- a willingness to give honest feedback to the team;

- a commitment to prayer – helpers pray together before each session and invite the prayer support of the whole congregation for themselves and the children and teachers who come to church;

- a commitment to read the Bible, as the RE Active Church small group activities are based on Bible passages, which helpers are asked to read, reflect on and immerse themselves in.

This sounds a lot to ask, but RE Active Church helpers do not need to be expert theologians or perfect Christians! Being a Christian means asking God to help us be Christlike – to be Christ to others, to model Jesus for others.

It is recommended that new helpers shadow a small group before running one on their own.

Recruiting helpers

We recruit a range of helpers and currently have 15 members of the congregation on the team. We have people to call on should unforeseen events prevent helpers from attending their session. We are always on the lookout for new helpers because people move on or move away, although a few of our helpers have been with us since RE Active Church began in 2003.

When recruiting your team, try to recruit helpers of different ages to give the children a breadth of life experience. We recruit men and women but, in practice, most long-term helpers are retired women who feel comfortable and confident working with children. But we aim to enlist at least one man for each workshop, in order to provide a positive role model for boys and avoid the subliminal message that church is not for them.

We also have helpers who are mothers with young children, before they go back to work or have another baby, and students returning from college or university are a great resource as their terms are relatively short, although they may go off travelling or seek paid holiday jobs.

We benefit, too, from helpers who have been made redundant or young people not yet in work, including people interested in (re)training as teachers, as they can include helping with RE Active Church on their CVs.

Child Protection considerations

The Child Protection or Vulnerable Persons legislation is complicated and subject to change. Consult the designated person responsible for Criminal Records Bureau (CRB) checks in your church to ensure that you are up to date with the latest requirements, and ensure that the required checks are carried out.

Be aware of this issue and ensure that RE Active Church helpers are never on their own with any child and the schools' teachers and helpers are always present and responsible for the children.

Training and retaining RE Active Church helpers

Regarding training, it is recommended that helpers receive the material relating to the small group they will be running in advance of each workshop, along with the handout Notes for RE Active Church helpers (see Chapter 9), so that they can familiarize themselves with the topic, reflect on the Bible passage and pray for the session. It is also suggested that new helpers shadow experienced helpers.

As the extra person, the organizer can check on how the material is working in each small group and provide support and feedback.

The team can meet for feedback at the end of each workshop to review what worked well, what didn't, pupils' responses, difficulties and moments to celebrate. This is also an opportunity to pray together, give thanks and ask for God's help.

Diocesan and other training opportunities in children's work can be suggested to helpers as appropriate.

Regarding retaining helpers, we have found that each successful workshop inspires and encourages helpers to continue to be part of the team. The children's appreciation of their efforts is usually self-evident and the teachers also usually thank the team on behalf of the class at the end of a session. Also, the organizer and vicar or minister or ministry team write a card or send an email to thank each helper individually after each workshop. The thanks of the congregation is also included in the next newsletter or the notices. We also celebrate the workshops in church in the prayers of thanksgiving and by including written reports in the parish magazine, PCC and APCM and on the website.

We try to ensure that it is clear the feedback of each team member is valued. We have found that, by doing this, fellowship grows within the team as we plan, pray, rejoice, laugh and share our struggles and moans with one another. Simple things, like providing drinks for helpers during each session, the team organizer or helpers bringing in little treats such as mince pies, hot cross buns or home-made cakes, and the team eating together at our church's Thursday Lunches, help enormously too.

A note about photographs

While school staff may (and often do) take photographs of the children in their care on school visits to church (in line with their school's photographic policy), the RE Active Church team is unable to photograph children or display any photographs they may be given by the school in a public place.

What helpers get out of it

RE Active Church can be demanding, but most helpers also find it a very rewarding thing to be involved in. Here is a comment from a regular helper, one that is echoed by many others:

I find helping with the visits very rewarding. I like to feel part of a scheme that brings children into church who might never otherwise see the inside of a church. Also, it's very satisfying to hear the children talk about what they have done on previous visits when they are reminded by seeing something they worked on last time.

RE Active Church is a learning experience for adults and children alike. Presenting Christmas, Easter and the life and teaching of Jesus to children and answering their questions challenges Christians to think deeply about what we believe and why it matters. We avoid or explain 'churchy', 'jargon' words that Christians often take for granted, helping children to understand them, as well as gain a vocabulary and the confidence to talk about faith and spiritual experiences.

Keeping it simple does not mean 'dumbing down' or giving out a 'be nice to others and tidy your room' message. In every workshop we make it clear that we don't have all the answers to questions of faith, and not all Christians look at everything in the same way. Thus, helpers learn with and from the children, who often care deeply about justice and the future of the planet.

Helpers' and teachers' responsibilities

Teachers are always responsible for their classes, accompanied by their classroom assistants and parent helpers in different combinations. It is the teachers' responsibility to take children to the toilet, administer first aid, sort matters of discipline, count children in and out of church and so on, as they would at school or for any other visit.

Schools carry out detailed risk assessments before visits. This should not be a problem as the RE Active Church team should always be risk-aware when setting up activities. Bear in mind that:

- children should be instructed to walk, not run, as they enter and leave church and move around the small group activities;

- all craft activities need to be age-appropriate and supervised;

- any consumption of food or drink needs to be agreed with the teachers.

Equipment, resources and budget

RE Active Church costs relatively little to run. Our church, like most churches, is mindful of the budget, so the workshops have been developed with costs in mind:

- we rely on the church's photocopier and laminator to prepare materials;

- we use the church's microphone and CD player, plus, occasionally, a TV and DVD player, computer or projector;

- the best resource is undoubtedly our team of helpers!

The basic equipment required for each session really is basic. You will need:

- photocopied instructions for helpers and (usually) photocopied sheets of the craft activities;

- sticky blank labels and washable felt-tip pens to make name labels for each child;

- small (preferably) wrapped sweets for the children or their teacher to take away, related to the theme;

- posters, other visual aids in magnetic frames and display boards (if they cannot be borrowed, posters and puppets may be quite expensive to buy, so home-made alternatives can be used, such as a rat glove puppet made from a sock or a set of large pictures telling the Christmas or Easter stories made by children in previous holiday clubs, plus used Christmas cards and magazine pictures can be made into posters, and the Internet has a very large selection of free religious images – simply search for copyright-free images for Palm Sunday and so on);

- simple visual aids and props (it is often possible to borrow much of what you need from elsewhere in your church or from members of the congregation, a diocesan resource centre or even from the school visiting you; soft modelling dough can be made very cheaply[2] and you can shop around to get the best deals on items that you have to buy – we have found many bargains in local shops, with items much cheaper than they are in craft catalogues);

- it may be a good idea to encourage regular donations from members of the team and the wider congregation to the work of RE Active Church – this sounds unlikely, but it happened in our church without any prompting and we were left a small legacy by one of our first helpers.

That said, a budget for RE Active Church needs to be agreed at the start to cover items that need to be replenished, such as:

- stocks of paper, pens and labels;

- special craft items, such as googly eyes and polystyrene dishes;

- small wrapped sweets so each child has one as a gift to take away at the end of the workshops.

The last could be regarded as optional, but in practice it really is only a small cost as we look out for special offers ahead of workshops, and this gesture is always appreciated by the children.

Running a workshop

Beforehand

In the month before a school visits, the organizer needs to:

- check which craft materials and equipment are required for the workshop and ensure that they are available from the church, diocesan resource centre or school;

- put out requests to the congregation for materials in the newsletter;

- find any remaining resources locally or order them in plenty of time;

- arrange for craft templates to be cut out - in our church, this often takes place during midweek coffee mornings!

Creating the right ambience

- **Warmth** Churches have a bad reputation for being cold! Many are difficult to heat, but it is really important to ensure that the building is adequately heated for each school visit. Heating is one of the hidden costs of running RE Active Church.

- **Presentation** Great care is rightly taken to order a church in such a way that it is suitable for adult worship. In the same way, a well-thought-out presentation of the small-group spaces affirms the importance the church places on the children's visits. Visual materials can be laminated and posters displayed in magnetic picture frames or on boards. A strong visual focus in each small group generates immediate interest, stimulates the imagination and aids discussion.

- **Seating** Seats need to be set out in advance for each small group. Usually a circle of small chairs or the most comfortable church chairs works well, with rugs on the floor.

- **Spacing** Workshops only need space to accommodate one class at a time (usually 30 children, plus teachers and any school helpers). We space the four small groups of seven or eight children around the church, using the side chapels and the children's corner as well as the nave. Other churches could use a vestry, side room or hall.

4

RE Active Church resources
Essential elements

The RE Active Church workshop material is tailored to children in primary school Years 3-6, although this can be adapted for children at Key Stage 1 and those with learning difficulties (see Chapter 11). Familiarity with the Christian faith and life grows with termly visits to church over the four years of primary school. The four-year cycle of material can be reused, improved or changed as necessary. In 2010, we gave the introduction and plenary conclusion to the summer workshop a World Cup slant and, in 2012, will look to give it an Olympics twist. Please feel free to adapt the material to your own circumstances or to reflect national events.

The RE Active Church resources are set out in Part 2, but below are brief descriptions of what is included and what they are.

RE Active Church craft activities

In our first RE Active Church workshops, we gave the children clipboards and worksheets, with pictures to reinforce the theme, and asked them to jot down their ideas at the end of each small group activity. We realized afterwards that some of the children were struggling with spelling and writing – it was too much like school and detracted from the different experience of being in a church. So we introduced a craft activity, which the children clearly enjoyed, and left it to the teachers to do written follow-up work if they wanted to in the school classroom. It worked so well, we have followed this pattern ever since.

Each child works on a simple craft activity, which they add to in each small group, and take away with them at the end. This is all part of their engagement in active learning. Research suggests that we remember just 20 per cent of what we hear, but 80 per cent of what we do,[1] which is why RE Active

Church material includes craft, simple play scripts, quizzes, songs and stories to act out with props.

We hope, too, that by having something they have made to take home, the craft activity will connect the children's experiences in church with home and encourage families to talk about faith. Equally, in the plenary session, the children are encouraged to talk about what they have made and done in the workshop with their family and friends. When children go on school trips they expect to bring home a souvenir of their visit – the craft activity fulfils this role at no financial cost to the child!

The craft item may incorporate an invitation to forthcoming church events or a separate invitation may be given to the children. These include a related Bible text to colour (photocopiable templates are given in Chapter 10). Many of the children come to our church's Christmas Tree Festival and Christingle services, to Messy Church and the Rock Solid youth groups, but we have no way of knowing whether this is as a result of these RE Active Church invitations or other contacts. There has, however, been little response to invitations to Good Friday events and Easter services.

Taking it further

Mindful of the increasing use of technology, we intend to include the address of the church's website (and we will add the joint town churches' website when this is up and running) in the invitations, to help parents and children follow up their church experience.

RE Active Church gift

At the end of a party, children are usually given something to take away. Some party bags and going-home presents are very elaborate, but RE Active Church offers instead a simple gift to each child as they leave 'God's party'. This takes the form of a small (usually) wrapped sweet, which is related to the theme of the workshop, such as a gold chocolate coin at Christmas, a mini chocolate egg at Easter, a pig-shaped sweet in the summer (linking with the story of the prodigal son).

This inexpensive gift is a reflection of God's generosity and welcome, an affirmation that each child is special. It helps to counteract the stereotype that God is a spoilsport or killjoy and reinforces the message that, like us, Jesus enjoyed parties and good times with his friends. Mindful of potential risks, however, we always:

- provide an alternative sweet in case of allergies;
- ask the teachers to say when the children can eat the sweet – now, at school, at home;
- if requested, we give the sweets to the teacher to distribute at the end of the school day rather than to the children as they leave church.

RE Active Church songs

RE Active Church workshops include optional songs to reinforce learning and capitalize on children's love of rhythm and repetition. Suggestions are included in each workshop. Children should be given the choice not to sing because the words may be contrary to their faith belief.

RE Active Church displays

Each workshop produces a simple display to be left in church for the following Sunday or longer. This may be something the children have made, including requests for prayer, or a large version of their craft activity, with a brief explanation.

A display in church is a way of valuing both the schoolchildren and the helpers. It also informs the wider congregation of the work done with schools and encourages its future involvement and support.

Engaging the senses

Sight

Pictures, visual aids and props are important resources in RE Active Church. The materials used in the small groups include a wide range of pictures and other visual aids as a focus for the group, to contribute to the children's understanding and encourage imagination, questions and discussion.

Visual images help children explore and connect with the story. Some pictures we use are home-made, while others have been bought or borrowed from the diocesan resource centre or local schools. They include:

- the Benedictine Nuns of Turvey Abbey's poster series[2] 'Jesus Our Hope', 'Jesus Our Way', 'Jesus Our Light' (ten posters in each set) and posters by Sieger Köder[3] – these are quite expensive, but worth investing in;
- 'The Christ We Share'[4] – a varied collection of images of Jesus;
- laminated pictures made by children in our holiday clubs;
- posters made from clip art or copyright-free images found by searching the Internet;
- displays of Christmas cards illustrating different aspects of the story;
- laminated images from magazines, papers or calendars – for example, the *Church Times'* Easter photographs;
- copyright-free pictures from other sources, such as of the Oberammergau[5] Passion Play;
- fuzzy-felt board and shapes.

Hearing

Music is usually played as the children enter and leave the church, as part of the whole experience. This includes Christmas carols, Easter hymns, traditional organ or choral music, modern worship songs, reflective Celtic instrumental music or Taizé chants. Also, there is scope in the plenary session to include a song if this is thought appropriate – some suggestions are included in the details for the workshops and the at-a-glance summary charts in Chapter 8.

Many primary school children are used to singing in lessons and assemblies. Singing is another way of reinforcing the learning from the workshop, especially if it is an action song. We may choose a song the children know or teach them a new one or join in with a piece of well-known secular music, such the *Friends* theme tune for our Easter friends workshop. We use a CD to sing along to if we do not have a competent singer on the team, and enlist the teachers' help too.

Engaging the other senses

There are fewer opportunities to engage with smell and taste, but these are included when possible in workshops - such as burning incense and sharing unleavened bread (after an assessment of dietary risks and with staff supervision).

The variety introduced by plays, quizzes, acted stories and open questions nurtures children's imagination and empathy. Short times of silence, too, allow time for children to reflect and respond either quietly or with a practical action.

Using technology

Over 97 per cent of households in Britain have a television,[6] and most children have one of their own or access to a computer and phone at home. Computers are also regarded as essential to teaching in twenty-first-century UK schools.

Using modern technology in RE Active Church can challenge the stereotype that churches are dated and unattractive. Alternatively, not using modern technology as a resource can reinforce the distinctive character of church and offer alternative ways of exploring a theme. In practice, however, the choice may come down to the technology available in a church and the availability of people to operate it.

At present, we use a variety of low-tech resources. The workshops can easily be adapted, however, to include PowerPoint presentations or film clips - short clips from *The Miracle Maker*, Story Keepers, *The Lion, the Witch and the Wardrobe*, *Finding Nemo* and the Harry Potter films, for example. We also use PowerPoint presentations using 'The Brick Testament' (Bible passages illustrated by Lego building-brick characters and scenes),[7] and find it helpful for displaying the words of songs in the plenary session. Otherwise, we choose not to rely on technology, but have given children the opportunity to work with a range of other materials.

Using the resources

The material used in the four small groups can be photocopied from Chapters 5, 6 and 7 on to four separate pieces of A4 paper or thin card. You may wish to enlarge the font and laminate the sheets or put them in clear pocket folders for helpers to refer to if needed in each workshop. The materials for each workshop can be kept and reused on a four-year cycle.

The helpers need to have copies of the material for the small groups they will be running ahead of the workshop so that they can familiarize themselves with it (see Recruiting a team, page 16, and Recruiting helpers, pages 17-18).

Format for each workshop

- The leader introduces and concludes each workshop, so needs to be familiar with the introduction and conclusion material. This can be photocopied or read from this book.

- The templates for the craft activity need to be photocopied and the various pieces cut out as indicated in Chapter 10.

- All the equipment needed is listed at the start of each workshop - this needs to be gathered together in good time beforehand.

- You will need to set up four small-group areas around the church - the specific materials needed for each group are listed at the top of the text for each workshop in Part 2, along with the visual focus for each group.

- Each workshop follows a common structure - a five-minute welcome and introduction by the leader to the whole class at the front of the church, four ten-minute activities in small groups in different parts of the church, and a fifteen-minute plenary conclusion by the leader with the whole class, again, at the front of the church.

- The extra helper (see pages 16-17) keeps time and uses a buzzer or bell to tell the helpers and children when they need to move on to the next small group.

- The children make name labels in the first small group and build up their craft item as they move around the four groups.

- As the children leave (see page 22 for other options), they are each given a small sweet, their craft item and an invitation to forthcoming church events.

Next, in Part 2, you will find all you need to run your own RE Active Church workshops.

Part 2
RE Active Church resources

5

Christmas

In each school year, the RE curriculum will probably build on what children already know about Christmas. In Hertfordshire (at the time of writing), Year 3 focuses on angels' messages; Year 4 Christmas celebrations; Year 5 Advent waiting and Jesus as the 'Light of the World'; Year 6 the importance of Christmas to Christians and what Christians believe about God. The topics covered in your local area will probably be similar.

This chapter sets out four one-hour workshops for Years 3-6 to explore Christmas in church:

- Christmas animals
- Christmas angels
- Christmas gifts
- Help! It's Christmas.

The teachers develop their own follow-up work for this workshop in school, according to their curriculum.

Workshop 1: Christmas animals

Overview of workshop See the at-a-glance summary, page 116.

You will need
- Timer.
- CD player.
- CD of Christmas carols, plus words and music, or CD of an optional song, such as 'Super Duper Christmas'[1] or 'Just Being Together'.[2]

For each class of 30: felt-tip pens, sticky labels, Christmas card templates to colour, Christmas decorations, tinsel and so on, small tables, 30 small chocolate coins.

For Group 1: small figures or pictures of Mary, Joseph and a donkey, large donkey puppet, toy or picture, Advent calendar.

For Group 2: small figures or pictures of Mary, Joseph and baby Jesus, large rat puppet (can be made from a sock), toy or picture.

For Group 3: small figures or pictures of shepherds, sheep and an angel, large sheep puppet, toy or picture.

For Group 4: small figures or pictures of wise men and a camel, large camel puppet, toy or picture.

Preparation Play the CD of carols as the children come in and leave. Set up four small-group areas, with the visual focus of Christmas decorations indicated in the materials for each group (see below). Photocopy the notes for the helpers and gather together all the other materials required.

Craft   The children colour in cards made from a sheet of A4 paper, folded, with the pictures on the outside and words on the inside (see template in Chapter 10). There is space to include the address of the church website (and joint town churches' website), if available, to help parents and children follow up the experience in church.

Leader   **Introduction to each class (5 minutes)**

(Welcome the children at the church door and lead them to the pews or seats at the front of the church. Invite them to put their coats and so on under the pews or seats to be collected at the end of the session.)

Welcome to our 'Christmas animals' workshop. Today we're asking you to be detectives. Your challenge is to find the characters in the Christmas story and see what you can learn from them.

Your teacher will put you into four small groups to go round each activity. The buzzer will tell us when to change.

We'll give you a sticky label to write your name on, so we know who you are – just your first name, as clearly as you can. The team members have their labels on already – let me introduce them to you now . . . You will also be given a Christmas card to add to as you go round each group *(show)*. There are four parts of the Christmas story to work on, based on our Christmas animals theme. We hope you'll show people at home your card and tell them what you did in church today.

Leader   **Conclusion to each session (15 minutes)**

We hid the figures/pictures of Mary, Joseph and so on in the Christmas decorations because it's easy to lose the meaning of Christmas in all the bits and pieces. It's easy to forget why we celebrate Christmas – the birth of Jesus, who is God with us. Jesus is the reason for the season. Jesus shows us what God is like and helps us be like him.

*(**Optional song**: 'Super Duper Christmas', 'Just Being Together', other.)*

(Collect the animal puppets, toys or pictures used in each small group to hold up to the class when mentioned during the following.)

I wonder what lessons we learned from the animals in the story . . . *(prompt if needed)*.

Like the donkey we can be . . . *(patient and willing to help)*.

Like the rat we can be . . . *(content, make the best of what we have)*.

Like the sheep we can be . . . *(generous and giving)*.

Like the camel we can . . . *(stick at things and not give up)*.

(Ask helpers for any interesting questions or comments.)

Thank you for working so well today. We'll leave the Christmas figures hidden in the decorations on a table in church so the congregation can see on Sunday what you have been doing with us. Enjoy your little chocolate coin when your teacher says you can eat it. Don't forget your invitation to *(mention any special Christmas services or events here)*. A Happy Christmas to you all.

Group 1: Mary, Joseph and the donkey (10 minutes)

Helpers should read the story beforehand in Luke 2.1–5.

Materials required   Pens, labels, Christmas card templates to colour, small figures or pictures of Mary, Joseph and a donkey, Christmas decorations, small table, large donkey puppet, toy or picture, Advent calendar.

Visual focus	Small table with Christmas decorations hiding Mary, Joseph and the donkey.
	With the first group, make a name badge – just their first name, written clearly – and write their full name on a Christmas card.
	Remember to keep ideas simple for Years 3 and 4, but expect more discussion with Years 5 and 6.
Helper	Mary, Joseph and their donkey are hidden in the Christmas decorations. They're not easy to spot, but if you are good detectives, you will be able to find them . . .
	Let's sit down and you can tell me what you know about Mary, Joseph and the donkey – the start of the Christmas story. We'll use these figures/pictures to help us . . . *(Mention that Mary and Joseph live in Nazareth but have to go to Bethlehem to register for the census, to pay taxes to the Romans, who rule the country. It's a long way – 80 miles – a hard journey because Mary is expecting a special baby – Jesus.)*
	Now, we need you to hide them ready for the next group. *(Encourage the children to hide the figures of Mary, Joseph and the donkey.)*
	(Hold the large donkey puppet or toy.) Let's hear what the donkey has to say . . .

| **Donkey** | Hello everyone! I live in Nazareth in the stable next to Joseph's workshop. He's the village carpenter, you know. I carry wood for him. I never bite or kick, even though I have strong teeth and hooves. I do what I'm asked, I never complain or ask why. We donkeys are patient animals. We like to help. |
| | One day, my master – Joseph – puts his young wife – Mary – on my back. She's very heavy. We set off on a long journey. I don't know where we're going, I just plod patiently along. I'm dead tired when we get to Bethlehem. There are many people – we're lucky to find a stable. Mary and Joseph sleep in the stable with me – there's no room at the inn. I munch on hay and Mary gives birth to her baby – a beautiful boy they call Jesus. This is worth waiting for. A special night for us all. |

The donkey in the Christmas story is patient and willing to help. I wonder if you are patient and good at helping . . .

We do a lot of waiting before Christmas. I wonder if you have an Advent calendar to tell you how many days to go . . . *(Show Advent calendar.)*

Extra for Years 5 and 6 if needed

I wonder what we have to wait for besides Christmas . . . *(Mention birthdays, holidays, exam results, which school we're going to, what job we're going to do, who we're going to marry and be with . . .)*

Waiting is part of our lives. Jesus waits 30 years between when he's born and when he starts his work telling people about God. That's a long time. I wonder why we have to wait for things . . . *(To give us time to prepare, get ready, grow up and mature . . .)*

| **Helper** | **Activity** |
| | Colour the first part of the card, which shows Mary, Joseph and the donkey, (numbered 1). Is there anything you want to say or ask about the story? We may not have the answers, but we'll note down your questions. Some things about God are hard to understand. |

Group 2: Jesus is born in the stable (10 minutes)

Helpers should read the story beforehand in Luke 2.6–7.

Materials required   Pens, labels, Christmas card templates to colour, small figures or pictures of Mary, Joseph and baby Jesus, Christmas decorations, large rat puppet (can be made from a sock), toy or picture.

Visual focus   Small table with Christmas decorations hiding Mary, Joseph and baby Jesus.

With the first group, make a name badge – just their first name, written clearly – and write their full name on a Christmas card.

Remember to keep ideas simple for Years 3 and 4, but expect more discussion with Years 5 and 6.

Helper   Mary, Joseph and baby Jesus are hidden in the Christmas decorations. They're not easy to spot, but if you are good detectives, you will be able to find them . . .

Let's sit down and you can tell me what you know about the birth of Jesus – just this bit of the Christmas story. We'll use these figures/pictures to help us . . . (*Mention that Bethlehem is crowded with people coming to register for the census, to pay taxes to the Romans, who rule the country. Every inn is full. A kind innkeeper takes pity on Mary because she's expecting a baby, and lets Mary and Joseph stay in his stable with the animals. That night, Jesus is born. Mary wraps him in baby clothes (swaddling bands) and lays him in the manger – the animals' feeding trough – to sleep.*)

Now, we need you to hide them ready for the next group. (*Encourage the children to hide the figures of Mary, Joseph and baby Jesus.*)

(*Hold the rat puppet or toy or picture.*) Let's hear what the rat in the stable has to say . . .

Rat   Hello everyone! I wonder what you think about me. Some people don't like rats – they think we're dirty and disgusting and live in smelly places like sewers and rubbish dumps, but we rats are clean animals. We wash as often as you. We live where we feel safe, away from people who could harm us. Me and my family live in this stable. We eat food the other animals leave – we rats aren't fussy eaters, not like some people. We're not greedy either. We make the best of things, we're happy with what we have. We rats are never bored, we always find things to do, keeping our nests tidy, looking after our families, playing with our friends. If people were like us, the world would be a much happier place – but back to my story.

Last night I was in the stable, looking for food, when I got a big surprise! The innkeeper brought in two people called Mary and Joseph and their donkey. They looked really tired. In the night, Mary gave birth to a beautiful baby boy they call Jesus – the Saviour of the world. I had a close look at the baby. Mary saw me and smiled. What a special night.

I wonder what you think about rats . . .

Sometimes we're afraid of something or someone without even knowing much about it or them, but Jesus welcomes everyone. God has no favourites – everyone is special, everyone matters to God.

I wonder if you're like the rat in our story – if you're happy with what you have, if you make the best of things, if you keep busy? Maybe you get bored and want what your friends have . . . ?

Extra for Years 5 and 6 if needed

Adverts try to make us buy things. Do you think adverts tell you what to buy . . . ?

Helper	**Activity**
	Colour the second part of your card, which shows baby Jesus in the manger (numbered 2). Is there anything you want to say or ask about the story? We may not have the answers, but we'll note down your questions. Some things about God are hard to understand.

Group 3: Angels appear to the shepherds (10 minutes)

Helpers should read the story beforehand in Luke 2.8-20.

Materials required Pens, labels, Christmas card templates to colour, small figures or pictures of shepherds, sheep and an angel, Christmas decorations, small table, large sheep puppet, toy or picture.

Visual focus Small table with Christmas decorations hiding shepherds, sheep and an angel.

With the first group, make a name badge – just their first name, written clearly – and write their full name on a Christmas card.

Remember to keep ideas simple for Years 3 and 4, but expect more discussion with Years 5 and 6.

Helper Shepherds, sheep and an angel are hidden in the Christmas decorations. They're not easy to spot, but if you are good detectives, you will be able to find them . . .

Let's sit down and you can tell me what you know about the shepherds – just this bit of the story. We'll use these figures/pictures to help us . . . *(Mention that the shepherds live on the hillside, day and night, looking after the sheep. It's tough work, in wind and cold, away from families, keeping sheep safe from wild animals and thieves. That first Christmas night, an angel tells the shepherds about a special baby – God's son – born in Bethlehem. Jesus is the Messiah and Saviour of the world. Lots of angels fill the sky, singing glory to God and peace on earth. The shepherds leave their sheep to find the baby in the manger. They tell Mary about the angels and praise God for all they've seen and heard . . .)*

Now, we need you to hide them ready for the next group. *(Encourage the children to hide the figures of the shepherds, sheep and angel.)*

(Hold the large sheep puppet or toy.) Let's hear what the sheep has to say . . .

Sheep Hello everyone! People think sheep are silly animals – rushing about, chased by sheepdogs – or boring, just standing around eating grass. They're wrong!

What we sheep do is give – we're the most generous animals. We eat grass to grow thick, woolly coats for you. Every year a man with clippers cuts our wool to make your jumpers, coats, carpets, rugs, blankets and all kinds of things to keep you warm and comfortable and looking good. Some of us sheep give you milk. Cows' milk makes some people ill, but they can drink our milk instead. Some of our milk is made into delicious cheese. Like I said, sheep are generous and giving.

Last night something special happened. First one, then a whole host of angels came to our hillside to tell our shepherds about a new baby king. Our shepherds rushed off to see the baby straight away. They didn't take us with them, more's the pity, but I heard they took some of our wool to keep baby Jesus warm. Now they're telling everyone about the new baby king, Jesus.

I wonder what you think about sheep . . .

I wonder if you like giving presents and doing things for other people like the sheep in our story . . .

I wonder what we can give others every day . . . (Help, friendship, sharing . . .)

Extra for Years 5 and 6 if needed

I wonder if the shepherds were right to leave their sheep . . . What would you have done?

Helper	**Activity**

Colour the third part of your card, which shows a shepherd (numbered 3). Is there anything you want to say or ask about the story? We may not have the answers, but we'll note down your questions. Some things about God are hard to understand.

Group 4: The wise men come to Jesus (10 minutes)

Helpers should read the story beforehand in Matthew 2.1-18.

Materials required   Pens, labels, Christmas card templates to colour, small figures or pictures of wise men and a camel, Christmas decorations, small table, large camel puppet, toy or picture.

Visual focus   Small table with Christmas decorations hiding wise men and camel.

With the first group, make a name badge – just their first name, written clearly – and write their full name on a Christmas card.

Remember to keep ideas simple for Years 3 and 4, but expect more discussion with Years 5 and 6.

Helper   Three wise men are hidden in the Christmas decorations. They're not easy to spot, but if you are good detectives, you will be able to find them . . .

Let's sit down and you can tell me what you know about the wise men – just this bit of the story. We'll use these figures/pictures to help us . . . (Mention that the wise men in the East see a special star, telling of the birth of a king of the Jews. They make the long, tough journey, endure cold nights, hot days, are away from their families and risk being attacked by wild animals and thieves. They look in the royal palace in Jerusalem for the new king, but King Herod sends them to Bethlehem. They follow the star, find baby Jesus and give him gifts of gold, frankincense and myrrh. An angel warns them not to return to Herod, as they had agreed with him, because he plans to kill the baby king. Instead, they go home another way, full of joy.)

Now, we need you to hide them ready for the next group. (Encourage the children to hide the figures of the wise men.)

(Hold the large camel puppet or toy or picture.) Let's hear what the camel has to say . . .

Camel   Hello everyone! Have you met a camel before? People say we're bad-tempered, that we bite and spit. You'd be bad-tempered too, if you had to walk miles across burning sand, carrying heavy loads on your back. We camels have good points too, though. We can go days without food or drink. We don't give up, but keep going, day after day, however much we have to carry.

One day, my master and his friends – they're rich, wise men – loaded us up and rode us to places we'd never been before – far from our own country, to strange new lands – following a special star. Sometimes we'd rest, but then it was on again. We stopped at King Herod's palace in Jerusalem, but that wasn't the end of our journey. We followed the star to a small house in Bethlehem. My master and his friends went in, taking the special gifts we'd been carrying – gold, frankincense and myrrh. They talked about 'a newborn king, the Son of God'. They were full of joy. We went home a different way. It wasn't easy, but we camels always stick with the job we're given.

I wonder what you think about camels . . .

I wonder if you're like the camel in our story, a mix of good and bad points . . .

The camel keeps on going and doesn't give up. I wonder if there are things you need to stick at, keep working on, at school or home. . . . *(Maybe friends, family, people we find difficult, subjects we find difficult, like spellings, maths, sports . . .)*

Extra for Years 5 and 6 if needed

Many people make New Year's resolutions about things they want to work at or change in the coming year. Have you ever made a New Year's resolution . . . ? Was it easy to keep . . . ? You don't have to say anything, but you can if you wish.

Helper

Activity

Colour the last part of the card, which shows a wise man (numbered 4). Is there anything you want to say or ask about the story? We may not have the answers, but we will note down your questions. Some things about God are hard to understand.

Workshop 2: Christmas angels

Overview of workshop   See the at-a-glance summary, page 116.

You will need
- Timer.
- CD player.
- CD of Christmas carols, plus words and music or CD of an optional song, such as 'Here we go up to Bethlehem'[3] for Years 3 and 4 or 'The Virgin Mary had a baby boy'[4] for Years 5 and 6.

For each class of 30: felt-tip pens, sticky labels, angel outlines and invitations to services or events (see templates, Chapter 10), little chocolates.

For Group 1: pictures of the Annunciation from used Christmas cards displayed on a board or in a picture frame, two rolls of sticky tape, eight pairs of scissors, printed messages to Mary (see page 36), small bell, sweet paper, spoon in a mug, book, water, matches, coins, paper for tearing, empty drinks can.

For Group 2: pictures of the angel and Joseph displayed on a board or in a picture frame, optical illusion pictures in which two different images can be seen, such as a duck and rabbit,[5] also displayed on a board or in a picture frame, 2 rolls of sticky tape, 16 paper doily 'wings' (cut 1 round paper doily into 16 segments), glue.

For Group 3: pictures of angels and shepherds from used Christmas cards displayed on a board or in a picture frame, two rolls of sticky tape, 5 cm lengths of silver or gold tinsel, glue.

For Group 4: pictures of wise men from used Christmas cards displayed on a board or in a picture frame, two rolls of sticky tape, two sets of eight laminated mazes (hard and easy levels - see template, Chapter 10), damp cloths, gold or silver stars or pens.

Preparation

Play the CD of carols as the children come in and leave. Set up four small-group areas, with the visual focus of the pictures required in the list above of materials for each group - the Annunciation for Group 1 and so on. Photocopy the notes for the helpers, plus the messages to Mary (see below), and gather together all the other materials required. Also, use the angel template (see Chapter 10) to make a large, A3 angel to show the children in the workshop and display in church with an explanation, for the congregation to see on Sunday.

Craft

The children cut out and add to their angel outline (see template, Chapter 10) in each group. A separate invitation to church activities to colour may include the address of the church website (and the joint town churches' website) if available, to help parents and children follow up the experience in church.

Leader

Introduction to each class (5 minutes)

(Welcome the children at the church door and lead them to the pews or seats at the front of the church. Invite them to put their coats and so on under the pews or seats to be collected at the end of the session.)

Welcome to our 'Christmas angels' workshop. Today we're looking at Christmas with the help of angels. Angels speak to Mary, Joseph and the shepherds.

Has anyone been an angel at school or in church . . . ?

I wonder what angels are like . . . ? *(Listen to any suggestions, but don't add to them.)*

I wonder what angels do . . . ? *(Again, listen, but don't add anything.)*

We'll come back to this at the end of the session.

Your teacher will put you into four small groups to go round each activity. The buzzer will tell us when to change.

We'll give you a sticky label to write your name on, so we know who you are - just your first name, as clearly as you can. The team members have their labels on already - let me introduce them to you now . . . Our craft activity today is to make an angel a bit like this to take home and maybe put on your Christmas tree *(show large angel)*. You'll add to it as you go round each group. In the last group, you need to fold and stick it, to finish it off. We hope you'll show people at home your angel and tell them what you did in church today.

Leader

Conclusion to each session (15 minutes)

A lot happens in the Christmas story. Let's put the events in order. Hands up to tell me . . . *(Mary says 'yes' to having God's baby, Joseph marries Mary, the shepherds hear the news, the wise men get things wrong and put them right.)*

I wonder what you found out about angels, what they're like . . . ? (*Often male, like Gabriel, scary, they tell people 'Do not be afraid.'*)

What do angels do? (*God's helpers, messengers, sing praise to God, live with God in heaven.*)

There are angels in many Bible stories, not just the Christmas story. At Easter, angels in the tomb tell Jesus' friends he's alive. I wonder how you'd feel if you saw an angel? (*Maybe shocked, surprised, scared, special.*)

I wonder if you'd do what the angel told you to do.

Mary, the shepherds and the wise men do what the angels tell them, what God wants, but it's their choice. They can make up their own minds. Just like us. When we hear about Jesus, we can listen or ignore him. God lets us choose what we believe and how we live.

I've never seen an angel. I can't prove angels exist. I can't prove God exists because there's more to God than we can understand, however old or clever we are, but Christians believe that God is with us and helps us make the most of our lives. Today we're being God's angels, God's messengers and sharing God's story with you.

(*Ask helpers for any interesting questions or comments.*)

(**Optional song**: *for Years 3 and 4, 'Here we go up to Bethlehem', with actions; for Years 5 and 6, 'The Virgin Mary had a baby boy'.*)

Thank you for working so well today. We'll leave our big angel in church so the congregation can see on Sunday what you have been doing with us. Enjoy your little chocolate when your teacher says you can eat it. Don't forget your invitation to (*mention any special Christmas services or events*). A Happy Christmas to you all.

Group 1: Mary – saying 'yes' to God (10 minutes)

Helpers should read the story beforehand in Luke 1.26-38.

Materials required   Pens, labels, angel outlines, eight pairs of scissors, pictures from used Christmas cards of the Annunciation displayed on a board or in a picture frame, two rolls of sticky tape, printed messages to Mary (see page 36), small bell, sweet paper, spoon in a mug, book, water, matches, coins, paper for tearing, empty drinks can.

Visual focus   Pictures of the Annunciation displayed on a board or in a picture frame.

With the first group, make a name badge – just their first name, written clearly – and write their full name on an angel outline.

Remember to keep ideas simple for Years 3 and 4, but expect more discussion with Years 5 and 6.

Helper   Let's see how good you are at listening. I'm going to make some noises behind these pictures and you have to guess what the noises are. Please don't call out, but put up your hand, so everyone can have a turn. (*Suggested noises: ring the small bell, rustle the sweet paper, stir the spoon in the mug, tear some paper, turn the pages of the book, pour some water, strike a match, jangle some coins, squash a drinks can . . .*)

The Christmas story begins with a girl called Mary. Is anyone here called Mary . . . ?

Mary's an ordinary girl, a bit older than you, a teenager, living in Nazareth, engaged to marry Joseph, the village carpenter. One day, Mary hears some amazing news from God. How do we usually get news . . . ? *(TV, someone tells us, by phone, letter, texts, email . . .)*

I wonder if God sent Mary a letter like this . . . *(Show the printed messages to Mary below.)*

Dear Mary
You are going to have a baby called Jesus.
Love,
God

Maybe a text like this . . . ?

M. U R 2 B mum,
baby ID Jesus

Could it have been an email like this . . . ?

FROM: God
TO: Mary
Re: News

Hi Mary
Baby Jesus coming.
Best of luck,
God

No, none of these! God's special news needs a special messenger. So God sends the angel Gabriel to Mary. Gabriel says, 'Hi Mary! God's very pleased with you. Don't be afraid. God's chosen you to have his Son. You're to call him Jesus.'

I wonder how Mary feels about this message . . . *(Maybe surprised, scared, pleased, special, excited, puzzled.)*

Mary wonders how she can have a baby when she hasn't lived with Joseph. The angel tells her God's Holy Spirit will make it happen. It's a big decision, but Mary trusts God and says 'yes'. Nine months later, Mary has a baby boy and calls him Jesus, just as the angel told her.

Mary is only a teenager, but God needs her help. Whatever our age, we can be like Mary. We can share God's work of caring for the world and for other people. Do you think we should do this . . . ?

I wonder how God speaks to us today . . . *(Through the Bible, when we pray, via that little voice inside us – our conscience, which is God advising us what we ought and ought not to do.)*

Helper	**Activity 1**

Look at the pictures of Mary and the angel Gabriel. I wonder which ones you like and why . . .

Helper	**Activity 2**

Cut out the angel. *(With the last group, curve the skirt of the angels round and stick the sides together to form a conical shape.)*

Is there anything you want to say or ask about the story? We may not have the answers, but we'll note down your questions. Some things about God are hard to understand.

Group 2: Joseph - seeing differently (10 minutes)

Helpers should read the story beforehand in Matthew 1.18-25.

Materials required   Pens, labels, angel outlines, scissors, 16 paper doily wings, glue, 2 rolls of sticky tape, pictures of the angel and Joseph displayed on a board or in a picture frame, optical illusion pictures in which two different images can be seen, such as a duck and rabbit,[6] also displayed on a board or in a picture frame.

Visual focus   Pictures of the angel and Joseph displayed on a board or in a picture frame and optical illusion pictures displayed on a separate board or picture frame.

With the first group, make a name badge - just their first name, written clearly - and write their full name on an angel outline.

Remember to keep ideas simple for Years 3 and 4, but expect more discussion with Years 5 and 6.

Helper   Some pictures can be viewed more than one way. I wonder what you can see in these pictures . . . *(Go round the group.)*

When we know there's another way of looking at it, we can see a different picture. We can help each other see what we missed - like the angel helps Joseph see things differently in the Christmas story.

I wonder what you know about Joseph . . . *(Joseph's a carpenter in Nazareth, engaged to marry Mary. Before they live together, Joseph finds Mary's going to have a baby. Joseph knows he's not the father.)*

I wonder how Joseph feels . . . *(Maybe surprised, angry, hurt, let down.)*

If Joseph reported Mary, she could be stoned to death. Joseph is a kind man and he loves Mary very much. I wonder what Joseph decides to do . . .

Joseph decides not to make a fuss. He decides not to marry Mary, but let her leave Nazareth quietly. Then an angel speaks to Joseph in a dream. The angel tells Joseph not to be afraid to marry Mary - her baby is God's son. They must call him Jesus, which means 'God saves', because he will save people from their sins. I wonder how Joseph feels now . . . *(Maybe surprised, pleased, special, scared, excited.)*

The angel helps Joseph see things differently. Joseph listens and does what the angel asks. He marries Mary and they call the baby Jesus.

Sometimes we need to be like Joseph - open to new ideas, willing to see things differently. I wonder if you can think of things people once thought were right, but we now think are wrong . . . *(Give clues if needed, for example, punishing children with the cane at home or in school, children being seen and not heard, children being thought of as not important, men (boys) thinking that they are better than women (girls), owning slaves, fighting between Christians - such as when Protestants fought Catholics - fighting people of other faiths - such as the Crusades, Christians v. Muslims - white people thinking they are superior to other races . . .)*

I wonder if it's easy to see things differently and be open to new ideas . . .

Helper   **Activity**

Stick the doily wings on to the angel outlines. *(With the last group, curve the skirt of the angels round and stick the sides together to form a conical shape.)*

Is there anything you want to say or ask about the story? We may not have the answers, but we'll note down your questions. Some things about God are hard to understand.

Group 3: Shepherds – sharing good news (10 minutes)

Helpers should read the story beforehand in Luke 2.8–20.

Materials required Pens, labels, angel outlines, pictures of angels and shepherds, from used Christmas cards displayed on a board or in a picture frame and 5 cm lengths of silver or gold tinsel, glue, two rolls of sticky tape.

Visual focus Pictures of angels and shepherds displayed on a board or in a picture frame.

With the first group, make a name badge – just their first name, written clearly – and write their full name on an angel outline.

Remember to keep ideas simple for Years 3 and 4, but expect more discussion with Years 5 and 6.

Helper I wonder if you can pass on a message without words. You can take it in turns to mime or act the activity I whisper to you. The rest of the group have to guess what it is – but remember: you're not allowed to speak.

A clue – all the activities are things people do at Christmas. It's OK to call out when you've guessed. *(Suggested actions: making a cake, wrapping a present, writing cards or a letter to Santa, decorating the tree, putting up decorations, singing carols, visiting friends, pulling a cracker.)*

Do you know who are the first people to hear that Jesus has been born? *(The shepherds.)*

I wonder how the shepherds found out? *(God sends angels to tell them.)*

Do the angels mime their message, like we've been doing? *(No, the angels sing loudly for the shepherds to hear.)*

This is the angel's message. Maybe one of you can read it *(Luke 2.10–12, NRSV, paraphrased)*:

> Do not be afraid, I have good news for you and for all people. God's special king, the Messiah, is born to save you. You'll find him, a tiny baby, lying in a manger.

I wonder how the shepherds feel when they hear this. *(Maybe scared, surprised, excited, pleased, special.)*

The shepherds rush to Bethlehem to find the stable and baby Jesus for themselves, but this isn't the end of the shepherds' story. What do you do with exciting news? *(Tell other people, share it with your friends.)*

That's what the shepherds do with their exciting news too. They tell everyone they meet about this special baby, Jesus, who is God with us.

Let's be like the shepherds. Let's pass a message all around our circle: 'Jesus is born! God is with us!'

Extra for Years 5 and 6 if needed

I wonder why God wants the shepherds to be first to know about Jesus. Shepherds at that time were very ordinary, working people who couldn't read or write. They were not important or rich people. *(God shows us that ordinary, poor, uneducated people matter – everyone is special to God.)*

Helper   **Activity 1**

Look at these Christmas cards of the shepherds. I wonder which ones you like and why . . .

Helper   **Activity 2**

Stick a piece of tinsel on to make the angel's halo. *(With the last group, curve the skirt of the angels round and stick the sides together to form a conical shape.)*

Is there anything you want to say or ask about the story? We may not have the answers, but we'll note down your questions. Some things about God are hard to understand.

Group 4: The wise men get it wrong and put it right (10 minutes)

Helpers should read the story beforehand in Matthew 2.1–18.

Materials required   Pens, labels, angel outlines, silver and gold stars or pens, two rolls of sticky tape, pictures from used Christmas cards of wise men, two sets of eight laminated mazes (hard and easy levels – see template, Chapter 10), damp cloths.

Visual focus   Pictures from used Christmas cards of wise men displayed on a board or in a picture frame.

With the first group, make a name badge – just their first name, written clearly – and write their full name on an angel outline.

Remember to keep ideas simple for Years 3 and 4, but expect more discussion with Years 5 and 6.

Helper   *(Hand out the laminated mazes – use the harder ones with Years 5 and 6. The children complete them with felt-tip pens, then wipe them clean with the damp cloths.)*

When you follow a maze, you can take wrong turns as well as follow the right path. It was like that for the wise men in the Christmas story. I wonder what you know about the wise men . . . *(Include that the wise men study the stars; the new bright star meant a new king of the Jews had been born; they pack precious gifts and follow the star to where the Jews live, the Holy Land.)*

I wonder where you'd expect a new king to be? *(A royal palace.)*

The wise men think so too. They stop following the star and go to King Herod's palace to ask him about the new king. I wonder what King Herod thinks about a new king. *(Maybe he is surprised, feels threatened, angry, frightened.)*

Herod doesn't want a new king, he wants to go on being king himself. If you were King Herod, I wonder what you would do next. Herod plans to find the new king and kill him. He tells the wise men, 'When you find this king, come and tell me and then I can worship him too.' Herod's evil plan doesn't work though. The wise men follow the star and find Jesus in Bethlehem. They give Jesus their gifts and go home a different way because God warns them in a dream not to return to Herod. An angel also warns Joseph about Herod's evil plan. Joseph escapes with Mary and baby Jesus into Egypt.

Extra for Years 5 and 6 if needed

Actions have consequences. What we do affects other people. If we don't listen or don't do what we're told, people can get hurt. I wonder if you can think of any examples . . . *(Playing with fire, road safety, stranger danger, pollution.)*

When the wise men go to King Herod's palace instead of following the star, Herod finds out about Jesus and plans to kill him. God, however, helps the wise men put things right. The wise men listen to God in a dream and don't go back to Herod. God can help us too – when we get things wrong, he can help us put things right. God forgives us and gives us a fresh start.

Helper	**Activity 1**

Look at these pictures of the wise men. I wonder which ones you like and why . . .

Helper	**Activity 2**

Decorate your angels with the gold and silver stars or use the gold and silver pens to draw stars on your angels. *(With the last group, curve the skirt of the angels round and stick the sides together to form a conical shape.)*

Is there anything you want to say or ask about the story? We may not have the answers, but we will note down your questions. Some things about God are hard to understand.

Workshop 3: Christmas gifts

Overview of workshop   See the at-a-glance summary, page 116.

You will need

- Timer.
- CD player.
- CD of Christmas carols, plus words and music or CD of an optional song, such as 'The Little Drummer Boy' or a verse and chorus of 'We Three Kings'.

For each class of 30: felt-tip pens, sticky labels, Christmas card templates to colour, Christmas crib with wise men, table, A3 sheet of paper or card with the words 'The wise men looked for Jesus. Wise men and women seek him still', little chocolates.

For Group 1: crown, cloak, sword, money bags, Sieger Köder or other Nativity picture displayed on a board or in a picture frame, glue sticks, small gold paper squares to stick on the king marked 'G' on the Christmas cards (see template, Chapter 10).

For Group 2: joss sticks or scented candle, matches, frankincense or a picture of some, pictures of Jesus ('The Christ We Share'[7] or ones you've collected) displayed on a board or in a picture frame, glue sticks, small sticky dots and rectangles to stick on the king marked 'F' on the Christmas cards (see template, Chapter 10).

For Group 3: four scented candles (for example, Christmas spices, rose, chocolate, pine), a pot of myrrh or picture of some, an outline picture of a sad face (just two dots for eyes and a downward curve for a sad mouth) on a paper plate, a small table.

For Group 4: map of the world or globe, pictures from used Christmas cards of the wise men displayed on a board or in a picture frame.

Preparation

Play the CD of carols as the children come in and leave. On a table, set up the Christmas crib with the wise men as a whole-class visual focus for the children during the introduction and conclusion to the session. Alongside it, place the A3 sheet of paper or card with the words 'The wise men looked for Jesus. Wise men and women seek him still'. Set up four small-group areas with the visual focus as indicated in the materials for each group (below). Photocopy the notes for the helpers and gather together all the other materials required.

Craft

The children colour and stick shapes on an A5 card with the template picture of the wise men (see template, Chapter 10) and invitation to church activities on the back. On the inside is a text to colour. You may include the church website (and joint town churches' website), if available, to help parents and children follow up the experience in church.

Leader

Introduction to each class (5 minutes)

(Welcome the children at the church door and lead them to the pews or seats at the front of the church. Invite them to put their coats and so on under the pews or seats to be collected at the end of the session.)

Christmas presents remind us of the wise men's gifts to Jesus. We're going to find out more about the wise men and their gifts today.

Your teacher will put you into four small groups to go round each activity. The buzzer will tell us when to change.

We'll give you a sticky label to write your name on, so we know who you are – just your first name as clearly as you can. The team members have their labels on already – let me introduce them to you now . . . You will also be given a Christmas card to add to as you go round each group *(show)*. We hope you'll show people at home your card and tell them what you did in church today.

Leader

Conclusion to each session (15 minutes)

It's a tradition to decorate Christmas trees at Christmas. I wonder why . . . *(A Christmas tree is evergreen, which means its leaves don't die, and this reminds us of God's everlasting love and eternal life with God.)*

I wonder what you put on your tree and why . . . *(Include:*

- *a star – reminds us of the wise men looking for Jesus;*
- *an angel – because an angel tells the news of Jesus' birth;*
- *lights – 'Jesus is the light of the world', he shows us how to live;*
- *shiny baubles – remind us of the wise men's gifts to Jesus;*
- *tinsel – reminds us of God's glory.)*

The wise men's gifts tell us about Jesus. I wonder if you remember what the three gifts mean . . .

- gold – Jesus is a king, the king of love, the king of all people;
- myrrh – Jesus is going to die for us;
- frankincense – Jesus is Emmanuel, God with us.

The wise men's gifts point to Easter:

- Jesus is mocked on the cross as King of the Jews;
- myrrh is used for his burial;
- on Easter Day, Jesus rises to new life and people worship him.

The wise men bring precious, expensive gifts to Jesus, but I wonder what we could give him . . . including simple gifts that please God and don't cost anything. *(Hugs, smiles, thank yous, helping and looking after people, thinking how others feel.)*

God is pleased when we give these simple gifts. We can give them every day too, not just on Christmas Day.

We give Christmas presents to our family and friends. I wonder if we can give Christmas presents to people we don't know, people who need help . . . *(Shoeboxes to Samaritan's Purse, money to charities.)*

God is pleased when we help other people. Jesus says that when we help other people, we are helping him.

(Ask helpers for any interesting questions or comments.)

*(**Optional song**: 'The Little Drummer Boy' or verse and chorus of 'We Three Kings'.)*

Thank you for working so well today. We'll leave the different pictures of Jesus in church so the congregation can see on Sunday what you have been doing with us. We hope you'll show people at home your card and tell them what you did in church today. Enjoy your little chocolate when your teacher says you can eat it. Don't forget your invitation to *(mention any special Christmas services or events as appropriate)*. Have a happy and caring Christmas.

Group 1: Gold for a king (10 minutes)

Helpers should read the story beforehand in Matthew 2.1-12.

Materials required   Pens, labels, Christmas card templates to colour, crown, cloak, sword, money bags, Sieger Köder or other Nativity picture displayed on a board or in a picture frame, glue sticks, small gold paper squares.

Visual focus   Nativity picture displayed on a board or in a picture frame.

With the first group, make a name badge - just their first name, written clearly - and write their full name on a Christmas card.

Remember to keep ideas simple for Years 3 and 4, but expect more discussion with Years 5 and 6.

Helper   I wonder who you think of when you hear the word 'king' . . . *(Prompt if needed - maybe famous kings in history, from stories, the Bible, such as Henry VIII, King Arthur, King Herod, King David.)*

I wonder what kings are usually like . . . *(Rich, powerful, have palaces or castles, armies, servants, fine clothes, jewels, crowns, lots of gold, even gold plates and cups.)*

I need someone to be a king today . . . *(Dress up a child with the crown, cloak, sword and money bags.)*

The rest of us can be the king's servants and bow or curtsey. I wonder if Jesus is this sort of king . . . *(Prompt if needed that, no, Jesus is poor, he talks about peace and love, serves people, he is not the king people expect, he's God with us, the Messiah, the King of Love, King of Kings, king of all people.)*

At Christmas, the wise men bring Jesus gold for a king. Let's hear the story from the Bible *(Matthew 2.1-11, NRSV)* - someone may like to read it:

> When they saw that the star had stopped, they were overwhelmed with joy. On entering the house, they saw the child with Mary his mother; and they knelt down and paid him homage. Then, opening their treasure chests, they offered him gifts of gold, frankincense, and myrrh.

It seems strange to find a king in a stable. I wonder why God wants Jesus to be born in a stable, not a royal palace . . . *(It shows that Jesus is a different king - he doesn't want people to wait on him, he comes to help us, not lord it over us. He's close to ordinary people - Jesus grows up to be a carpenter, he works for a living, like ordinary people do, he knows what ordinary life is like.)*

I wonder what Mary and Joseph think when they see the wise men and their presents . . . *(Maybe they were surprised even though the angels told them Jesus is God's Son, pleased, honoured.)*

People mock Jesus as 'King of the Jews' when he dies on the cross, but on Easter Day, Jesus rises to new life – he's king of all people.

Extra for Years 5 and 6 if needed

(Look at the Nativity picture.) I wonder what you can see . . . I wonder where you would be in the picture . . . *(In the Sieger Köder picture, some people worship Jesus, some people aren't interested. God doesn't force people to take notice of him. You can see three crosses and the 'INRI' on the manger that point to Easter. 'INRI' means 'Jesus King of the Jews' – the charge Pilate puts above the cross when Jesus dies.)*

Helper

Activity

Colour king G on your card. Stick on a gold present square. Is there anything you want to say or ask about the story? We may not have the answers, but we'll note down your questions. Some things about God are hard to understand.

Group 2: Frankincense for God (10 minutes)

Helpers should read the story beforehand in Matthew 2.1-12.

Materials required   Pens, labels, Christmas card templates to colour, joss sticks or scented candle, matches, frankincense or a picture of some, pictures of Jesus ('The Christ We Share' or ones you've collected) displayed on a board or in a picture frame, glue sticks, small sticky dots and rectangles.

Visual focus   Pictures of Jesus on a board or in a picture frame.

With the first group, make a name badge – just their first name, written clearly – and write their full name on a Christmas card.

Remember to keep ideas simple for Years 3 and 4, but expect more discussion with Years 5 and 6.

Helper   *(Light a joss stick or scented candle.)* This is like incense. I wonder what you know about incense . . . *(People use incense in the temple when they pray to God; it's expensive, strong-smelling, like prayers rising up to heaven.)*

I wonder if you've been anywhere where there's incense . . . I wonder how it makes you feel . . .

(Pass round the frankincense to see and smell and touch or show the picture.) This is frankincense – I wonder if you know what it is . . . *(The resin of a tree. The tree is cut to drain the sap, which hardens into 'tears' and is then collected.)*

Let's remind ourselves about frankincense in the Christmas story *(Matthew 2.1-11, NRSV)*. Someone may like to read it:

> When they [the wise men] saw that the star had stopped, they were overwhelmed with joy. On entering the house, they saw the child with Mary his mother; and they knelt down and paid him homage. Then, opening their treasure chests, they offered him gifts of gold, frankincense, and myrrh.

The wise men kneel down to baby Jesus. Who might you kneel down to . . . ? *(Maybe to kings and queens or in church to God.)*

Helper

Activity 1

Jesus is a special king. Jesus has a special name – Emmanuel, God with us. Jesus also shows us what God is like. We know about Jesus from stories in the Bible. There are no photographs or drawings of Jesus when he lived on earth, but people try to imagine what he's like. Look at the pictures of Jesus. Take your time. Find a picture you like, then we can talk about it together as a group if you want to . . .

Extra for Years 5 and 6 if needed

Older groups can also find a picture of Jesus they don't like or that surprises them.

Helper

Activity 2

Colour king F on your card. Stick on a little dot and rectangle to make a candle to remind you of incense. Is there anything you want to say or ask about the story? We may not have the answers, but we'll note down your questions. Some things about God are hard to understand.

Group 3: Myrrh for burial (10 minutes)

Helpers should read the story beforehand in Matthew 2.1-12.

Materials required Pens, labels, Christmas cards to colour, four scented candles (for example, Christmas spices, rose, chocolate, pine), a pot or picture of myrrh, outline picture of a sad face on a paper plate, small table.

Visual focus The pot or picture of myrrh displayed on a small table, together with the sad face.

With the first group, make a name badge – just their first name, written clearly – and write their full name on a card.

Remember to keep ideas simple for Years 3 and 4, but expect more discussion with Years 5 and 6.

Helper Different smells remind us of different things. *(Pass the scented candles round the circle.)* I wonder what you think each smell is and what it reminds you of. Just pass them round, then you can tell the group what you think.

Different smells remind us of different places or people. Some smells remind us of good times, some smells remind us of sad times. *(If you have one, pass round the pot of myrrh to see and smell; if not, point to the picture.)* This is myrrh. I wonder what you know about myrrh . . . *(It is an expensive perfume that was used to embalm people who've died. It was one of the wise men's gifts and points to Jesus dying at Easter on the cross and rising to new life. Like frankincense, myrrh is a resin, gathered by cutting the bark of a tree, letting the sap ooze out and dry, then collecting it.)*

I wonder what Mary and Joseph think about being given this present . . . *(Maybe surprised, sad, puzzled.)*

Sad things happen to people everywhere – they're part of every human life. I wonder if you've seen sad things on the news . . . *(Wars, natural disasters, such as earthquakes, tsunamis, tornadoes, floods, famines, plus poverty, murders.)*

You don't have to say anything, but I wonder if sad things sometimes happen to your family too . . . *(Friends let you down, pets die, people die, people move away.)*

Sad things happen to Jesus too. His friends let him down, people laugh at him, hurt him, kill him and bury him in a tomb. That's not the end of the story though. On Easter Day, Jesus rises to new life. Christians believe that, when we die, we will have new life with God.

God doesn't want us to afraid. I wonder if you can guess how many times the words 'Do not be afraid' appear in the Bible . . . The answer is 365 – that's one for each day of the year!

We can't see God but we believe God is always with us to help us in good times and in bad times. God is on our side. We can always trust God.

Activity

Colour king M on your card. Is there anything you want to say or ask about the story? We may not have the answers, but we'll note down your questions. Some things about God are hard to understand.

Group 4: Looking for Jesus (10 minutes)

Helpers should read the story beforehand in Matthew 2.1-12.

Materials required   Pens, labels, Christmas card templates to colour, map of the world or globe, pictures from used Christmas cards of the wise men displayed on a board or in a picture frame.

Visual focus   Pictures from used Christmas cards of the wise men displayed on a board or in a picture frame.

Remember to keep ideas simple for Years 3 and 4, but expect more discussion with Years 5 and 6.

With the first group, make a name badge – just their first name, written clearly – and write their full name on a Christmas card.

Remember to keep ideas simple for Years 3 and 4, but expect more discussion with Years 5 and 6.

Helper   I wonder how far you've travelled . . . maybe you can show the group on our map/globe.

I wonder how you got there, how long the journey took, why you made the journey . . .

We're going to hear about the wise men's journey from the Bible *(Matthew 2.1-2, NRSV)* – someone may like to read it:

> In the time of King Herod, after Jesus was born in Bethlehem of Judea, wise men from the East came to Jerusalem, asking, 'Where is the child who has been born king of the Jews? For we observed his star at its rising and have come to pay him homage.'

I wonder where the wise men came from . . . *(Somewhere in the East, we don't know exactly where.)*

I wonder how the wise men travelled . . . *(The Bible doesn't say, but camels were the usual transport – they were like cars are today.)*

I wonder how long it took them . . . *(The Bible doesn't say, but probably quite a long time – a week or more.)*

The wise men don't come at the same time as the shepherds, although we often put them together when we arrange a Christmas crib or on Christmas cards. It's tradition to keep our Christmas decorations up until Twelfth Night (called Epiphany), which is to remember that the wise men came twelve days after Christmas.

I wonder if it was a dangerous journey . . . *(Maybe they came across robbers, deserts and mountains; it would have been expensive and they had to leave their friends, families and work behind.)*

I wonder why the wise men went on such a long and dangerous journey with such expensive presents . . . *(The stars show them something special has happened and they want to pay homage to the new king. Jesus is a special king, he's God with us.)*

Let's hear more of the story from the Bible *(Matthew 2.9–11, NRSV)*. Maybe someone would like to read it:

> When they had heard the king [Herod], they set out; and there, ahead of them, went the star that they had seen at its rising, until it stopped over the place where the child was. When they saw the star had stopped, they were overwhelmed with joy. On entering the house, they saw the child with Mary his mother; and they knelt down and paid him homage. Then, opening their treasure chests, they offered him gifts of gold, frankincense, and myrrh.

I wonder how the wise men feel when they see baby Jesus . . . *(Full of joy, awe, wonder, glad the journey's over, maybe surprised, puzzled, maybe full of questions.)*

I wonder why God guides the wise men to Jesus . . . *(Shows Jesus is for all people, not just the Jews; for rich, educated people as well as poor, uneducated shepherds.)*

Extra for Years 5 and 6 if needed

I wonder if the story is what you expected – there are no kings, no stable and no camels mentioned; the Bible doesn't say three people, just three presents!

I wonder why the wise men are sometimes called kings . . . *(Maybe because the gifts are so expensive; the prophets said kings would come to Jesus.)*

Helper **Activity 1**

Look at these pictures of the wise men from Christmas cards. Some of them show wise men or kings at different ages, from different countries. I wonder why . . . *(Shows Jesus is for all people, all races, not just Jews; for all ages of life, young, middle-aged and old; God has no favourites, he cares for everyone.)*

Helper **Activity 2**

Look inside your card. It says, 'The wise men looked for Jesus. Wise men and women seek him still.' I wonder what you think about this . . . We can talk about it as you colour the words. Is there anything you want to say or ask about the story? We may not have the answers, but we'll note down your questions. Some things about God are hard to understand.

Workshop 4: Help! It's Christmas

Overview of workshop See the at-a-glance summary, page 116.

You will need
- Timer.
- CD player.
- CD of Christmas carols, plus words and music, or CD of an optional song, such as 'We wish you a Merry Christmas'.

For each class of 30: felt-tip pens, sticky labels, Christmas card templates to colour, a filled shoebox (such as for Samaritan's Purse), large Turvey[8] or other Christmas pictures (see what is needed for each group below).

For Group 1: large picture of the journey to Bethlehem (Turvey or other), pictures of refugees from newspapers and magazines laminated into a poster, strips of paper, glue sticks, sand.

For Group 2: Nativity set (optional), large picture of the Nativity in the stable (Turvey or other), large cardboard box, a Christingle candle collection box or equivalent from charities supported by your church, nice small box with a 'Thank You' label stuck on to it, 30 small pieces of paper, glue sticks, pieces of straw.

For Group 3: large picture of the shepherds (Turvey or other), 60 small, wrapped hard sweets, Christmas wrapping paper, sticky tape, cotton wool, glue sticks.

For Group 4: large picture of the wise men (Turvey or other), 30 sticky stars, A3-size home-made picture of Jesus with the words 'Where did I say that you should buy so much stuff to celebrate my birthday?',[9] 30 blank gift tags and 30 strands of wool, each 30 cm long.

Preparation

Play the CD of carols as the children come in and leave. Set up four small-group areas, with the visual focus as indicated in the materials for each group (below). Photocopy the notes for the helpers and gather together all the other materials required.

Craft

The children colour and add to an A5 card made with the template pictures (see Chapter 10). Inside is an invitation to church activities with space to include the address of the church website (and joint town churches' website), if available, to help parents and children follow up the experience in church.

Leader

Introduction to each class (5 minutes)

(Welcome the children at the church door and lead them to the pews or seats at the front of the church. Invite them to put their coats and so on under the pews or seats to be collected at the end of the session.)

Welcome to our 'Help! It's Christmas' workshop. Some people panic about Christmas, about how much they have to do before the 'big day'. Other people have different worries, like finding enough to eat or a place to sleep. Millions of people around the world and in this country need help.

We're going to look at the first Christmas, some 2,000 years ago, and find out what Christmas is really about.

Your teacher will put you into four small groups to go round each activity. The buzzer will tell us when to change.

We'll give you a sticky label to write your name on, so we know who you are – just your first name as clearly as you can. The team members have their labels on already – let me introduce them to you now . . . You will also be given a Christmas card to add to as you go round each group *(show),* with invitations to our special Christmas services and activities. We hope you'll show people at home your card and tell them what you did in church today.

Leader

Conclusion to each session (15 minutes)

A lot happens in the Christmas story. We'll put the events in the right order using our Christmas pictures. Put your hands up to tell me the order . . . *(Journey, stable, shepherds, wise men.)*

Adverts make us think Christmas is about getting big presents, including stuff we don't need, but the Christmas story begins with giving. God so loved the world he gave us Jesus, to show us how to live with him and with other people in his world.

Inside your card, to remind you, you'll see the words, 'God so loved the world that he gave his only Son'.

God gives us the gifts we need to be truly happy – gifts like love, joy and peace. God wants us to be like him and give gifts to other people. Your small groups looked at people who need help and gifts we can give them. *(Adjust as necessary to relate to your own church.)* Put up your hands to tell me . . .

(Group 1 – shoeboxes for refugees

Group 2 – Christingle candles for homeless children

Group 3 – sweets for people who get left out

Group 4 – using our gifts for others.)

Giving to other people, doing things for others, makes us happy and makes them happy too. We can't solve all the problems refugees and homeless people have, but we can do our bit to help. We can do what we can – like in the story of the starfish.

Thousands of starfish are washed up on a beach and dying in the hot sun. A boy begins to pick them up and throw them back into the sea. A man walking along the beach is puzzled. 'Why bother throwing the starfish back? There are thousands of them. You can't save them all.' The boy looks at the starfish in his hand. 'There are thousands', he says, 'I can't help them all, but I can make a difference to this one.' He throws it back into the sea and carries on saving as many starfish as he can.

We end now singing new words to a song I think you know – 'We wish you a merry Christmas':

> Our gifts we all bring, to Jesus the king
> We wish you a merry Christmas and a Happy New Year.

(Ask helpers for any interesting questions or comments.)

Thank you for working so well today. We'll display your paper chains and 'Thank You' box in church so the congregation can see on Sunday what you have been doing with us. Enjoy your sweet when your teacher says you can eat it, and enjoy giving the other one you wrapped to someone else. Don't forget your invitation to *(mention any special Christmas services or events here, as appropriate)*. A Happy Christmas to you all.

Group 1: Mary and Joseph – leaving home (10 minutes)

Helpers should read the story beforehand in Luke 2.1–5 and Matthew 2.13–15.

Materials required   Pens, labels, Christmas card templates to colour, large picture of the journey to Bethlehem (Turvey, for example), pictures of refugees from newspapers and magazines laminated into a poster, filled shoebox (such as for Samaritan's Purse), strips of paper, glue sticks, sand.

Visual focus   Large picture of the journey to Bethlehem.

With the first group, make a name badge – just their first name, written clearly – and write their full name on a Christmas card.

Remember to keep ideas simple for Years 3 and 4, but expect more discussion with Years 5 and 6.

Helper

I wonder if you've packed for a journey – maybe a school trip or holiday . . . You can't take everything with you, can you?

I wonder what you miss most when you go away from home . . . *(Your bed, bedroom, favourite toys, TV, computer games, pets, friends, family.)*

In the Christmas story, Mary and Joseph go on a long journey . . . *(Show the large picture.)* I wonder what you know about Mary and Joseph and their journey . . . *(Include the Roman census, to pay taxes, journey from home in Nazareth to home town of Bethlehem, Mary engaged to Joseph, expecting a baby, probably travelling by donkey, although it doesn't say so in the Bible.)*

I wonder what Mary and Joseph take on their journey to Bethlehem . . . *(Maybe money, bread, cheese, wine, fruit, clothes, baby clothes, blankets.)*

(For Years 3 and 4.) We'll go round the circle. Repeat what other people say and add an item to the list. I'll start us off: 'We're on a journey to Bethlehem with blankets . . .' next person: 'We're on a journey to Bethlehem with blankets and bread . . .' and so on.

Extra for Years 5 and 6 if needed

This isn't the only journey Mary and Joseph make. After Jesus is born Mary and Joseph go to Egypt. I wonder if you know why . . . *(Include: Joseph is warned by an angel in a dream to go to Egypt to escape King Herod, who wants to kill the new baby king, and Herod's soldiers kill all the baby boys under two years old in Bethlehem.)*

Like Mary and Joseph, many people today have to leave their homes. I wonder what people run away from . . . *(Wars, floods, famine (food shortages), hurricanes, tornadoes, volcanoes, bad governments.)*

(Show the poster of refugees.) Refugees can't take much with them. They miss their homes, families, friends and jobs; they often live in crowded tents, cold in winter, hot in summer. I wonder how you'd feel if you were a refugee . . . *(Afraid, bored from waiting around, worried about people left behind, worried about food, clothes, water, medicines, doctors, missing your job or school.)*

At church, at Christmas we fill shoeboxes for asylum seekers, refugees, victims of famine and war, to let them know we care about them. Has anyone filled shoeboxes at school, Brownies or Beavers, home . . . ? *(Show and talk about what's inside a shoebox.)*

God wants us to care for other people and share what we have with people in need. Maybe you can fill a shoebox too.[10]

Helper

Activity 1

A paper chain reminds us we're part of the human family. Write your name on a paper strip and join it to the big chain to leave in church.

Helper

Activity 2

Spread glue and sprinkle sand on your card to remind you of Mary's and Joseph's journey. Colour the first part of your card (numbered 1). Is there anything you want to say or ask about the story? We may not have the answers, but we'll note down your questions. Some things about God are hard to understand.

Group 2: The innkeeper makes room (10 minutes)

Helpers should read the story beforehand in Luke 2.6-7.

Materials required   Pens, labels, Christmas card templates to colour, Nativity set (optional), large picture of the Nativity in the stable (Turvey or other), large cardboard box, nice small box with a 'Thank You' label stuck on to it, 30 small pieces of paper, glue sticks, pieces of straw, Christingle candle collection box, if using.

Visual focus   Large picture of the Nativity in the stable, plus Nativity set, if using.

With the first group, make a name badge – just their first name, written clearly – and write their full name on a Christmas card.

Remember to keep ideas simple for Years 3 and 4, but expect more discussion with Years 5 and 6.

Helper   I wonder if you know where you were born – maybe at home or in a hospital . . .

Jesus wasn't born at home or in a hospital. I wonder where Jesus was born . . . *(Include: in Bethlehem, where Mary and Joseph go to register for the census, there's no room at the inn, the innkeeper lets Mary and Joseph stay in the stable.)*

(Show the large picture of the Nativity in the stable.) I wonder what it's like in the stable. Let's close our eyes and imagine we're in the stable with Mary and Joseph. Is it dark inside . . . ? What kind of light is there . . . ? What can you smell . . . ? Is it warm or cold . . . ? Where can you sleep . . . ? Where can you eat . . . ? Is it a good place to have a baby . . . ?

Christmas crib scenes look nice, but I wouldn't want to sleep in a stable. It's not clean or comfortable. I wonder why God chooses to be born in a dirty stable, not a royal palace . . . *(Shows what God is like, God is with ordinary people in ordinary places, God doesn't mind mess, Jesus comes to serve others, not to be served.)*

Some people are homeless and sleep on the streets in shop doorways and eat food from dustbins. Maybe you've seen them . . . *(Hold the large cardboard box.)* I wonder what it's like to sleep in the open, with a cardboard box or newspaper to cover you. I wonder how you'd feel . . . *(Cold, afraid, sad, lonely, hungry, dirty, bored.)*

The innkeeper doesn't know Mary and Joseph, but he knows they need help and he does what he can, like the people who help with Crisis at Christmas.[11] Do you know what Crisis at Christmas do . . . ? *(Offer a warm place to sleep homeless people, collect and give them food and clothes, baths and medical care over Christmas.)*

What about the rest of the year? *(Some people try to help homeless people all year round with soup and sandwiches, drop-in centres and hostels to care for them and help them build a new and better life.)*

Some children in this country are homeless too. Every five minutes a child in the UK runs away from problems at home.[12] I wonder if you know what this is. *(Show Christingle candle collection box – if you collect for another charity at Christmas, show an object associated with that charity and adapt the following accordingly.)* We fill these candles with money for the Children's Society to help runaway children return home or find new homes.

Helper   **Activity 1**

We don't always realize how lucky we are to have a loving family, a safe home, clean water on tap, toilets, food in our fridges and cupboards, toys, clothes we can choose to wear, to go to school, see a doctor when we're sick . . . millions of people in our world don't have these things. *(Hold the 'Thank You' box and hand out a small piece of paper to each child.)* Draw or write something or things on your piece of paper that you know you are lucky to have, then put it in our 'Thank You' box to leave in church.

Helper **Activity 2**

Here's a challenge: can you remember to say 'Thank you' every day for at least one meal?

Helper **Activity 3**

Colour the manger on your card (numbered 2). Stick on some pieces of straw. Is there anything you want to say or ask about the story? We may not have the answers, but we'll note down your questions. Some things about God are hard to understand.

Group 3: The shepherds aren't left out (10 minutes)

Helpers should read the story beforehand in Luke 2.8-20.

Materials required Pens, labels, Christmas card templates to colour, large picture of the shepherds (Turvey or other), 60 small, wrapped hard sweets, Christmas wrapping paper, sticky tape, cotton wool, glue sticks.

Visual focus Large picture of the shepherds.

With the first group, make a name badge - just their first name, written clearly - and write their full name on a Christmas card.

Remember to keep ideas simple for Years 3 and 4, but expect more discussion with Years 5 and 6.

Helper I wonder if some people have to work when we're asleep and at weekends . . . *(Doctors, nurses, carers, firefighters, police officers, train drivers, farmers, fishing crews, shop workers, lorry drivers.)*

In the Christmas story, the shepherds live out on the hillside, looking after their sheep day and night. I wonder what it would be like to be a shepherd . . . *(Rough, cold, sometimes dangerous, wild animals, thieves, lonely away from home and families, not well paid.)*

I wonder what you know about the shepherds in the Christmas story . . . *(Hold the large picture of the shepherds and piece the story together. Include that angels tell them God's special baby, Jesus the Messiah, has been born in Bethlehem, and lies in a manger, and how they go to see for themselves, praise God and tell everyone they meet about the new baby king.)*

The shepherds are the first to hear about Jesus. I wonder why God chooses shepherds to be the first to hear his special news . . . *(Shows ordinary people matter to God, God includes everyone, God has no favourites.)*

God doesn't want the shepherds to miss out. I wonder if some people miss out today - at school or in our town . . . *(Some children don't have many friends, older people may live on their own or in care homes and be lonely, have no family.)*

I wonder what we can do for them . . . *(Look out for them, try to include them.)*

Helper **Activity 1**

Each wrap up two sweets in Christmas paper - one for you to eat when your teacher says you can and one to give to someone who might be feeling left out. Please take them home and ask who you might give one to - maybe a relative, neighbour . . .

Helper

Activity 2

Colour the sheep part of your card (numbered 3). Stick on cotton wool for the sheep's wool. Is there anything you want to say or ask about the story? We may not have the answers, but we'll note down your questions. Some things about God are hard to understand.

Group 4: The wise men - sharing our gifts (10 minutes)

Helpers should read the story beforehand in Matthew 2.1–12.

Materials required   Pens, labels, Christmas card templates to colour, large picture of the wise men (Turvey or other), 30 sticky stars, A3-size home-made picture of Jesus with the words, 'Where did I say that you should buy so much stuff to celebrate my birthday?', 30 blank gift tags and 30 strands of wool, each 30 cm long.

Visual focus   Large picture of the wise men.

With the first group, make a name badge - just their first name, written clearly - and full name on their Christmas card.

Remember to keep ideas simple for Years 3 and 4, but expect more discussion with Years 5 and 6.

Helper   Some presents are just fun, some are practical and useful. I wonder what's your best ever present . . .

In the Christmas story, there are some very special presents . . . *(Piece together the story with the children using the large picture of the wise men.)*

I wonder why we have presents at Christmas . . . *(Remember to include the wise men's gifts to Jesus and God's gift to us - Jesus.)*

Jesus is God's special gift to us. Jesus doesn't stay a baby - he grows up and shows us what God is like, he tells stories, he makes sick people well, he forgives people, he changes lives, he dies on the cross and rises to new life at Easter to save us from death and sin (selfishness).

(Look at the picture of Jesus with the words, 'Where did I say that you should buy so much stuff to celebrate my birthday?') I wonder if we get too many presents at Christmas . . . *(Talk about the top Christmas gifts and suggest some simple gifts instead.)*

Helper

Activity 1

Colour the star on your card (numbered 4). Stick on a star.

Helper

Activity 2

On a gift tag, write your name, another person's name and something simple you could give them or do for them as a Christmas present. Thread some wool through the hole in the tag, knot the ends and take it home to put on your tree, ready to give someone for Christmas.

Helper

Activity 3

Ask at home if you can give good-quality toys you no longer play with to a charity shop or appeal.

Is there anything you want to say or ask about the story? We may not have the answers, but we'll note down your questions. Some things about God are hard to understand.

6
Easter

In each school year, the RE curriculum will probably build on what children already know about Easter. In Hertfordshire (at the time of writing), Year 3 focuses on how Christians celebrate Easter; Year 4 the Last Supper and Easter food; Year 5 the events of Holy Week; Year 6 the importance of Easter to Christians today and questions relating to suffering. The topics covered in your local area will probably be similar.

This chapter sets out four one-hour workshops for Years 3–6 to explore Easter in church:

- Easter footprints
- Easter words
- Easter friends
- Eggy Easter.

The teachers develop their own follow-up work for this workshop in school, according to their curriculum.

Workshop 1: Easter footprints

Overview of workshop   See the at-a-glance summary, page 117.

You will need
- Timer.
- CD player.
- CD of Easter or general songs, plus words and music (for example, 'The Best Worship Songs . . . Ever' boxed sets, traditional hymns, Handel's *Messiah*, other oratorios, Out of the Ark Music).
- Brown X on an A4 sheet of card.

For each class of 30: felt-tip pens, sticky labels, Easter spinners to colour, fasteners, large pictures of Palm Sunday, Maundy Thursday (washing of the feet), Jesus' arrest, Good Friday, Easter Day,[1] Jesus and Peter by Sea of Galilee (Turvey[2] or other), mini chocolate eggs.

For Group 1: 8 copies of play (see below), 16 palm leaves cut from A4 green paper, donkey puppet (optional), hymn books.

For Group 2: bowl of warm water, vacuum flask with hot water, towel, paint in a tray with a sponge, lining paper.

For Group 3: cockerel toy or picture of one (optional), quiz.

For Group 4: toy caterpillar, cloth bag, toy butterfly (placed in the bag), knitted or toy Jesus, white cloth, shoebox, 2p coins, tomato sauce, saucers, wipes.

Preparation   Play the CD of Easter or general songs as the children come in and leave. Set up four small-group areas, with the visual focus as indicated in the materials for each group (see below). Photocopy the notes for the helpers and gather together all the other materials required.

Craft

The children make an Easter spinner from the circles in the templates (see Chapter 10). The first is printed on one side and one section needs to be cut out. The second circle is printed on both sides. The top side has pictures to colour and the back includes an invitation to the Easter activities and space to include the address of the church website (and joint town churches' website), if available, to help parents and children follow up the experience in church. The children colour different parts of the spinner as they go round the small groups, then, at the end, lay the circle with the cut-out section on top of the second circle, pictures side up, aligning the edges, and push a fastener through the centre. The top circle can now be rotated to show the different pictures on the circle below in the 'window', and the invitation can be seen on the back of the spinner.

Leader

Introduction to each class (5 minutes)

(Welcome the children at the church door and lead them to the pews or seats at the front of the church. Invite them to put their coats and so on under the pews or seats to be collected at the end of the session.)

Welcome to our 'Easter footprints' workshop. Put up your hands if you follow a football team . . . a singer or group . . . if there's a TV programme you can't miss . . . We all follow something.

Today we're following Jesus in the Easter story and asking why people still follow Jesus.

Your teacher will put you into four small groups to go round each activity. The buzzer will tell us when to change.

We'll give you a sticky label to write your name on, so we know who you are – just your first name as clearly as you can. The team members have their labels on already – let me introduce them to you now . . . You will also be given two circles and a fastener pin to make into an Easter spinner *(show)*. There are four different parts of the Easter story to colour, based on our Easter footprints theme. We hope you'll show people at home your spinner and tell them what you did in church today.

Leader

Conclusion to each session (15 minutes)

Hold up your spinners . . . They look great! If you haven't finished colouring them, you can do so at school or at home.

(Hold up the brown X on the sheet of card.) If you get an 'X' in a birthday card or text message, what does it mean? *(Love.)*

When I was at school, our teachers put a red cross, 'X', on work we got wrong. I'm told you sometimes get a green cross, 'X', now – is that right? *(Check beforehand what the school's practice is.)* So a cross also means something's wrong.

If I turn this brown 'X' this way round *(so it forms a plus, '+')*, it looks like the cross Jesus dies on, on Good Friday, like the crosses we see in church *(point to one)*.

Jesus dies on the cross because he loves us, this much *(extend your arms wide)*, and he wants to put right the things we do wrong.

Let's put the Easter story in order, using the pictures. The story begins on . . . *(Palm Sunday)* then . . . *(Maundy Thursday)* then . . . *(Jesus' arrest)*. That's not the end – there's . . . *(Good Friday)*.

Good Friday is not the end of Jesus – on Easter Day God raises Jesus to new life. Jesus brings new life to all his friends too.

Remember when Peter lets Jesus down and says he doesn't know Jesus? Peter feels really bad. After Easter, Jesus meets Peter by the Sea of Galilee (hold picture) and puts things right. Jesus asks Peter, 'Do you love me?' not once, but three times. I wonder why he asks him three times? (To cancel out Peter's three denials.)

Jesus forgives Peter and gives him a fresh new start, just as Jesus forgives us when we mess up, when we feel bad, when we're sorry. Jesus trusts Peter with a special job. Jesus tells Peter to 'feed my sheep', to carry on his work of helping people know God. Peter and the other disciples start telling the whole world about Jesus, like we're telling you about Jesus today.

(Go through any comments or questions the children have, such as, 'Why is it called Good Friday when Jesus dies?' It's 'God's Friday' and good comes out of Jesus' death - it means we can have new life with God now and when we die. There's no Easter without Good Friday! No celebration and no chocolate eggs, which are symbols of that new life!)

Thank you for working so well today. We're going to leave the Easter footprints sheet in church so the congregation can see on Sunday what you have been doing with us. We've got a little egg for each of you to take away to remind you of today. Don't forget your invitation to (mention any special Easter services or events here, as appropriate). A Happy Easter to you all.

Group 1: Palm Sunday and the donkey (10 minutes)

Helpers should read the story beforehand in Matthew 21.1-11.

Materials required   Pens, labels, Easter spinners to colour, fasteners, large picture of Palm Sunday, 8 copies of play, 16 palm leaves cut from A4 green paper, donkey puppet (optional), hymn books.

Visual focus   Large picture of Palm Sunday.

With the first group, make a name badge - just their first name, written clearly - and write their full name on a spinner.

Remember to keep ideas simple for Years 3 and 4, but expect more discussion with Years 5 and 6.

Helper   (Show large picture of Palm Sunday.) I wonder what's happening in this picture . . . ? I wonder if you know this story . . . How do you think Jesus looks . . . ? There are no wrong answers, just say what you think . . . (Sad, peaceful, confident, in charge, like or not like a king, ordinary, holy, kind.)

(Give out the parts and act out the play. See page 56 for the script.)

Helper   **Activity 1**

Colour the palm leaf, donkey footprint and 'Hosanna!' on your spinner. 'Hosanna' means 'save us'. Does the story surprise you? Is there anything you want to say or ask about the story? We may not have the answers, but we'll note down your questions. Some things about God are hard to understand.

Helper   **Activity 2**

Christians say 'Hosanna' to Jesus in our hymns, songs and prayers. You may know some songs . . . (For example, 'Give me joy in my heart', 'Hosanna'. If you have time, give the children hymn books and let them find a hymn with 'Hosanna' or their favourite hymns.)

Palm Sunday play

(based on Matthew 21.1-11)

(You will need an adult narrator and children to play Jesus, a disciple, donkey (a non-speaking part, but child can hold donkey puppet, if using), the crowd, holding the paper palm leaves, and people of Jerusalem (these last two groups are the remaining children and helpers). Stand in a big circle to read. The helper guides the children as they read.)

Narrator	Long ago, the prophets said God would send Israel a king. He would ride into Jerusalem on a donkey. Jesus and his friends, the disciples, are outside the city of Jerusalem.
Jesus	Go to the next village and bring me the donkey tied up there.
Disciple	Just take it? What if someone asks what we're doing?
Jesus	Tell them, 'The Lord needs it. He'll send it back soon.'
Disciple	*(leads in the child who is the 'donkey', holding the donkey puppet, if using)* Here's the donkey, Jesus. We'll use our coats to make a saddle *(use a jumper).*
Narrator	Jesus sits on the donkey. *(Jesus walks slowly behind the donkey across the circle.)* The crowd and people of Jerusalem spread their coats on the road and put branches from palm trees in front of Jesus. *('Crowd and people of Jerusalem' each lay down one of their paper palm leaves.)*
Crowd	*(say loudly, waving their second leaf)* Hosanna! Hosanna! Thank God for his king! *(Repeat, even louder.)*
Narrator	Jesus rides into Jerusalem on the donkey.
People of Jerusalem	Who is this man?
Crowd	He's Jesus, the prophet from Nazareth in Galilee.

Extra for Years 5 and 6 if needed

I wonder why the crowd shout 'Hosanna'. What do they want Jesus to save them from? *(The Romans, poverty, sickness, evil.)*

Group 2: Maundy Thursday and the washing of the feet (10 minutes)

Helpers should read the story beforehand in John 13.2-17.

Materials required Pens, labels, Easter spinners to colour, fasteners, large picture of Maundy Thursday (washing of the feet), bowl of warm water, vacuum flask with hot water, towel, paint in a tray with a sponge, lining paper.

Visual focus Large picture of Maundy Thursday (washing of the feet).

With the first group, make a name badge – just their first name, written clearly – and write their full name on a spinner.

Remember to keep ideas simple for Years 3 and 4, but expect more discussion with Years 5 and 6.

Helper *(Show large picture of Maundy Thursday.)* I wonder what's happening in the picture. I wonder if you know this story. *(Prompt if necessary.)* Jesus eats a special meal called . . . *(the Last Supper)* with his friends on the night before he dies, which we call . . . *(Maundy Thursday)*. Jesus washes his friends' feet before they eat, which was the job of . . . *(the lowest person – a slave or servant, not a teacher or leader like Jesus).*

I wonder how Peter feels about this . . . *(Confused, surprised, indignant, worried, wants to stop Jesus.)* He doesn't want Jesus to wash his feet because . . . *(Jesus is important, he's the teacher and leader.)* Jesus insists on washing Peter's feet, though, to set an example of . . . *(How to be a leader who serves and cares for others.)*

Jesus and his disciples eat . . . *(bread and wine)*, as Christians do in church in our service of . . . *(Holy Communion or Mass or the Lord's Supper or the Eucharist – different churches give the service different names.)*

How do you think Jesus looks? Remember, there are no wrong answers . . . *(Focused, concentrating, sad, kind, caring, humble, ordinary, like Peter, in control.)*

We need a volunteer to make a footprint in paint for our poster. We'll display your and the other footprints in church with the words 'Love and serve' and a note of explanation. *(Put one child's foot in the paint, then press it down on the paper. The child then hops to a chair to sit down. Each group adds one footprint to the paper, so at the end there are four footprints.)*

Our volunteer needs his/her foot washed now – is anyone willing to kneel and wash his/her foot . . . or would you like me to do it for you?

(Talk about being a leader like Jesus, who serves, cares for others, keeps people safe, helps them, teaches them.) Are there leaders like Jesus who work for the good of others, who look after others in school, at home, in the world . . . ? *(Maybe teachers, parents, class representatives, school's head boy or girl, prefects (as appropriate), football and netball team captains, maybe Gandhi, Mother Teresa.)*

Your school looks after everyone in it and helps people in need too. I wonder what your school does for . . . *(Red Nose Day, Children in Need, special appeals, people in the local community.)*

When we care for other people, we're following Jesus. This Church . . . *(Mention any activities the church does, such as collects money for different projects, visits people who are sick at home or in hospital, provides a weekly lunch club; maybe point out displays around the church about them.)*

Helper   **Activity**

Colour in the footprint, 'Love and serve' and the bowl of water on your spinner. Does the story of the Last Supper surprise you? Is there anything you want to say or ask about the story? We may not have the answers, but we'll note down your questions. Some things about God are hard to understand.

(Note: in our first workshop, each child walked in the paint and we washed everyone's feet. The children loved it, but it took too much time.)

Group 3: Good Friday and the cockerel (10 minutes)

Helpers should read the story beforehand in Matthew 26.69-75.

Materials required   Pens, labels, Easter spinners to colour, fasteners, large picture of Jesus' arrest, cockerel toy or picture of one (optional), quiz.

Visual focus   Large picture of Jesus' arrest.

With the first group, make a name badge - just their first name, written clearly - and write their full name on a spinner.

Remember to keep ideas simple for Years 3 and 4, but expect more discussion with Years 5 and 6.

Helper   *(Show picture of Jesus' arrest.)* I wonder what is happening in the picture . . . I wonder if you know the story.

How do you think Jesus looks? Remember, there are no wrong answers . . . *(Calm, sad, lonely.)*

After the Last Supper, Jesus takes his friends to a quiet place to pray - the Garden of Gethsemane. His friend Judas comes with guards to arrest Jesus and take him away. Jesus' friends panic and run away. Peter is scared, but he follows Jesus to see what happens next. Later, a servant girl sees Peter and says, 'You're one of Jesus' friends.'

Does Peter say:

(a) 'Yes, I'm his best friend.'

(b) 'I don't know what you're talking about.'

(c) 'It's not me - it's that man there.'

(Let the children choose and give their reasons for their decisions.)

Another girl sees Peter and says, 'This man was with Jesus.' Does Peter say:

(a) 'I swear, I don't know Jesus.'

(b) 'I've met Jesus, but he's not my friend.'

(c) 'Yes, I was with Jesus.'

(Let the children choose and give their reasons.)

Then, one of the crowd says to Peter, 'You are one of Jesus' friends - you speak like him, you're from Galilee too.' Does Peter say:

(a) nothing and walk away

(b) 'Jesus is my friend and I'll stand by him.'

(c) 'I really swear, I don't know this Jesus.'

(Let the children choose once more and give their reasons, then continue with the story.)

Peter says that he doesn't know Jesus three times. A cockerel crows *(show cockerel toy or picture, if using)* and Peter remembers Jesus' words: 'Before the cock crows you will deny me three times.' Peter is so upset, he weeps.

The soldiers take Jesus away. They beat him, laugh at him and make him carry a heavy cross to the place where he will be killed. The crowds shout 'Crucify, crucify him!'

I wonder how Peter feels.

I wonder how Jesus feels.

I wonder if you would always stand by your friends.

Remember, say what you really think - there are no wrong answers!

Extra for Years 5 and 6 if needed

In some countries today it's hard to follow Jesus. Christians are put in prison and sometimes killed. Churches are closed, burnt down or bombed. Do you think you would stand up for what you believe if it put you and your family in danger?

Helper	**Activity 1**

Colour the cockerel footprint, 'Crucify him!' and the cross on your spinner. As you colour, think about people hurting us when they say bad things or let us down . . . times we hurt other people and let them down . . . *(they can share aloud if they wish).*

Helper	**Activity 2**

Spend a few minutes in silence and think about these questions. Can you forgive someone who has hurt you? Do you need to say sorry to someone . . . or to God? God always forgives us and gives us a new start.

Is there anything you want to say or ask about the story? We may not have the answers, but we'll note down your questions. Some things about God are hard to understand.

Group 4: Easter Day and a butterfly (10 minutes)

Helpers should read the story beforehand in Matthew 28.1-9.

Materials required Pens, labels, Easter spinners to colour, fasteners, large Easter Day picture, toy caterpillar, cloth bag, toy butterfly (placed in the bag), knitted or toy Jesus, white cloth, shoebox, 2p coins, tomato sauce, saucers, wipes.

Visual focus Large Easter Day picture, caterpillar and butterfly.

With the first group, make a name badge - just their first name, written clearly - and write their full name on a spinner.

Remember to keep ideas simple for Years 3 and 4, but expect more discussion with Years 5 and 6.

Helper *(Show the children a grubby 2p coin, then put it in some tomato sauce on a saucer. Tell them we'll find out why you've done this at the end. Show them the toy caterpillar.)*

I wonder what happens to a caterpillar . . . (As they tell you, wrap it up in cloth bag, to act as a cocoon.)

The cocoon looks dead, but out of it comes new life – a beautiful butterfly. (Pull the toy butterfly out of the bag.) It's surprising but true – has anyone seen it for themselves?

The caterpillar and butterfly remind us of Easter. (Show the large Easter Day picture.) I wonder what is happening in the picture . . . I wonder if you know the story . . . (Piece it together with them. Jesus dies on the cross. His friends wrap his body in a cloth and bury him in a tomb that's like a cave. They roll a huge stone in front to seal the tomb and go home. They know he's dead. Early on Easter morning, some of Jesus' friends go to the tomb to anoint his body with expensive oil as a sign of love. They find the stone has been rolled away, the tomb is empty and Jesus is alive.) I wonder how Jesus' friends feel . . . Remember, say what you think – there are no wrong answers. (Surprised, happy, confused, afraid, doubting.)

How do you think Jesus looks in the picture? Can you see the marks of the nails on his hands and feet?

(Use the knitted or toy figure of Jesus to reinforce key points of the story.) Jesus really does die on the cross; he's wrapped in white cloth (wrap up figure) and put in a tomb (shoebox). Then, three days later, on Easter Day, the tomb is empty and Jesus meets his friends; he's very much alive (take Jesus out of the cardboard-box tomb, fold the cloth up and leave it in the box). Only the grave clothes remain in the tomb. Easter surprises everyone. Jesus really is alive.

After Easter, Jesus is the same, but different. Like our coin. (Take the coin out of the tomato sauce and wipe it clean.) Our coin is shiny. It's the same coin, but it's different, better than before. After Easter, Jesus is the same, but different. He dies on the cross and rises to new life so he can be with us always and we can have new life with God.

Jesus brings out the best in us, he helps us be kind and loving, not just thinking about ourselves. Jesus forgives us when we mess up and gives us a new start. We can be like the coin. We can be clean and new.

We can't see Jesus now, but Christians believe Jesus is with us always. We can see the difference Jesus makes to our lives and to other people.

Helper

Activity

Colour the butterfly, 'He is risen!' and the empty tomb on your spinner. (Talk about butterflies being used at Easter as a picture of resurrection and new life.) Does the Easter story surprise you? Is there anything you want to say or ask about the story? We may not have the answers, but we'll note down your questions. Some things about God are hard to understand.

Workshop 2: Easter words

Overview of workshop   See the at-a-glance summary, page 117.

You will need
- Timer.
- CD player.
- CD of Easter or general songs, plus words and music (for example, 'The Best Worship Songs . . . Ever' boxed sets, traditional hymns, Handel's *Messiah*, other oratorios, Out of the Ark Music), plus optional song, 'Celebrate', if using.

For each class of 30: felt-tip pens, sticky labels, polystyrene dishes, invitations, large pictures of Palm Sunday, the Last Supper, Good Friday, Easter Day (pictures of the Oberammergau Passion Play, or another) and a flower cross, four envelopes, four sets of the words 'Hope', 'Love', 'Forgiveness', 'New life', 'JOY' printed out on card, two small sticks or strips of card to form a cross, chocolate Easter egg, Easter cards, mini chocolate eggs.

For Group 1: a small pile of stones.

For Group 2: rug or 8 cushions to sit on, low table, cloth for table, 16 plastic cups, big jug of red drink, flat bread, 8 tea towels, 8 large elastic bands or bands made from the legs of tights to fit a child's head, bowl of water, towel, 60 squares of silver foil (7 cm × 7 cm) and a chalice and plate ready-made (see instructions, Activity 3, below), 60 tiny bits of Blu-Tack, an actual chalice and plate with bread and wine.

For Group 3: straws, scissors, sticky tape, hot cross buns, eight photocopied scripts for the play in plastic wallets or on card, eight baseball hats - labelled 'Jesus', 'Priest', 'Thief 1' and 'Thief 2' and four marked 'Crowd' (optional).

For Group 4: green soft modelling dough,[3] 30 small stones, 30 flowers to colour, 30 cocktail sticks, sticky tape, bulb, pot, pot of flowers, Easter cards.

Preparation

Play the CD of songs as the children come in and leave. Set up four small-group areas, with the visual focus as indicated in the materials for each group (see below). Photocopy the notes for the helpers and gather together all the other materials required.

Craft

Using the template as an example (see Chapter 10), the children make mini Easter gardens in the polystyrene bowls. There is also a template for a separate invitation to church activities with space to include the address of the church website (and joint town churches' website), if available, to help parents and children follow up the experience in church.

Leader

Introduction to each class (5 minutes)

(Welcome the children at the church door and lead them to the pews or seats at the front of the church. Invite them to put their coats and so on under the pews or seats to be collected at the end of the session.)

Welcome to our 'Easter words' workshop. We're going to find out about Easter and what it means.

Your teacher will put you into four small groups to go round each activity. The buzzer will tell us when to change.

We'll give you a sticky label to write your name on, so we know who you are - just your first name as clearly as you can. The team members have their labels on already - let me introduce them to you now . . . We are going to be making little Easter gardens *(show template)* to remember the different parts of the Easter story. Each group will also have an envelope to collect an Easter word from each activity. We hope you'll show people at home your garden and tell them what you did in church today.

Leader

Conclusion to each session (15 minutes)

Hold up your Easter gardens - they look great!

Put up your hands to put the Easter story in the right order using the pictures, and tell us the words you've collected in each activity . . . *(Hope for Palm Sunday, love for Maundy Thursday, forgiveness for Good Friday, new life for Easter Day.)*

The words you collected summarize Easter. Easter is about hope, love, forgiveness and new life . . . and it's also about joy. *(Show word JOY.)* I wonder if you know what the letters 'J', 'O' and 'Y' stand for . . . 'J' is for 'Jesus first', 'O' is for 'others second' and 'Y' is for 'yourself last' – JOY.

Jesus tells us that the way to be happy is to think about God and other people, not just ourselves.

The cross reminds us of this. *(Show the two sticks or pieces of card.)*

(Show one of the sticks or pieces of card, holding it vertically.) This is me, thinking of myself, what I want.

(Hold the other stick or piece of card horizontally across the middle of the first one. Point to the horizontal stick and say . . .) This is me thinking about other people – how they feel, what they need. It makes a cross. Jesus teaches us to think about God and other people, not just ourselves. That is the way to be happy, to be full of JOY. You don't have to believe me – you can try it for yourselves and see.

Easter means new life for Jesus and for us. We eat chocolate Easter eggs *(show)* and send Easter cards *(show)* to celebrate new life. We make our church beautiful with lots of flowers. *(Show flower cross picture.)* Sometimes we cover a cross with flowers as a sign of new life coming out of Jesus' death.

(Ask helpers for any interesting questions or comments, such as, 'Why is it called Good Friday when Jesus dies?' It's because it's God's Friday and good comes out of Jesus' death – there's no Easter without Good Friday.)

*(**Optional song**: 'Celebrate'[4] or other, with actions.)*

Thank you for working so well today. We'll leave a big version of your Easter garden on a table in church so the congregation can see on Sunday what you have been doing with us. We've got a little egg for each of you to take away to remind you of today. We'll give your teachers a separate invitation to our special Easter services to give out in school. A Happy Easter to you all.

Group 1: Palm Sunday – hope (10 minutes)

Helpers read the story beforehand in Luke 19.28–40.

Materials required   Pens, labels, polystyrene dishes, large picture of Palm Sunday, a small pile of stones, printed word 'Hope'.

Visual focus   Large picture of Palm Sunday, a small pile of stones and the printed word 'Hope'.

With the first group, make a name badge – just their first name, written clearly – and write their full name on a dish.

Remember to keep ideas simple for Years 3 and 4, but expect more discussion with Years 5 and 6.

Helper   *(Arrange the pile of stones in the centre of where the children are to sit in a circle. Point to the stones.)* As we're talking, listen out and see if these stones make a noise.

(Show the large picture of Palm Sunday.) Our stones are part of this story. I wonder what's happening here . . . (Piece together the story of Palm Sunday – Jesus rides into the city of Jerusalem on a donkey, the crowds spread their coats on the road to make a special path, cut palm leaves from trees to wave, shout, 'Hosanna! Blessed is the one who comes in the name of the Lord!' (Mark 11.9, NRSV). Some Jewish leaders, called Pharisees, tell Jesus to stop the people shouting. Jesus says, 'if these [the people] were silent, the stones would shout out!' (Luke 19.40, NRSV))*

Did our stones make any noise . . . ? No, our stones don't need to make a noise because people *aren't* quiet – the crowd shouts out to Jesus, and Christians still sing songs of praise and tell people about Jesus, like we're telling you here today.

I wonder why the crowds cheer Jesus . . . *(They're excited, they think Jesus is the Messiah they've been waiting for, God's special king, a hero who will drive out the Romans and make Israel a great nation.)*

I wonder why the Jewish leaders, the Pharisees, want to stop people cheering Jesus . . . *(They don't think Jesus is the Messiah, God's special king, the one they've been waiting for.)*

Extra for Years 5 and 6 if needed

(Go through the following answers to the last two points above with older children. The prophets said Israel's king would come to Jerusalem riding on a donkey. God's chosen Messiah would save his people. Jesus has been healing the sick, telling wonderful stories, performing miracles, showing God's love to everyone. The people think, 'He must be the Messiah we've been waiting for.'

They're worried the Romans will punish the people. They think Jesus is wrong to call God his Father, to forgive people's sins and welcome outcasts and sinners. Jesus threatens the authority of the priests and Pharisees, the Jewish leaders.)

Helper

Activity 1

Here is the word 'Hope' and an envelope to put it in. It is your group's envelope to take to the next activity and add the next word to.

Helper

Activity 2

Draw a palm leaf on a sticky label to stick in your Easter garden dish.

Helper

Activity 3

I wonder what you hope for, for yourself or for the world. You can think about your hopes as you draw a palm leaf and stick it on your dish. If you want to, you can share your hopes with the group. Is there anything you want to say or ask about the story? We may not have the answers, but we'll note down your questions. Some things about God are hard to understand.

Group 2: The Last Supper – love (10 minutes)

Helpers read the story beforehand from Mark 14.22-23.

Materials required   Pens, labels, polystyrene dishes, large picture of the Last Supper, rug or 8 cushions to sit on, low table, cloth for table, 16 plastic cups, big jug of red drink, flat bread, 8 tea towels, 8 large elastic bands or bands made from the legs of tights to fit a child's head, bowl of water, towel, 60 squares of silver foil (7 cm × 7 cm) and a chalice and plate ready-made (see instructions, Activity 3, below), 60 tiny bits of Blu-Tack, printed word 'Love', actual chalice and plate with bread and wine.

Visual focus   Large picture of the Last Supper, printed word 'Love'.

With the first group, make a name badge – just their first name, written clearly – and write their full name on a dish.

Remember to keep ideas simple for Years 3 and 4, but expect more discussion with Years 5 and 6.

Helper

I wonder how people show us they love us, our family or friends . . . *(Tell us, look after us, give us hugs, kisses, presents, treats, spend time with us, play with us, share meals with us.)*

I wonder if you can remember any special meals you've shared with family and friends . . . *(Prompt if needed - birthdays, weddings, Christmas.)*

Jesus enjoys parties and meals with his friends too. On the night before he dies, Jesus shares a special meal with his friends. I wonder if you know what we call it . . . *(The Last Supper.)* You can share the Last Supper with me now. Take off your shoes and sit on the cushions around the table *(low table with the cloth on it, red drink, plastic cups, flat bread)*, put on your special headwear *(tea towels held in place with the elastic or bands made from tights)*. Now I'm going to wash your hands *(bowl of water and towel)*. A servant usually washed people's feet, but at the Last Supper, Jesus chose to do this job. I wonder why Jesus washes his friends' feet . . . *(They are dusty, to freshen up for the meal, gives us an example to follow - Jesus serves us as he wants us to be like him, to serve and care for other people.)*

Jesus eats a special Passover meal with his friends every year. There is lamb and bitter herbs, flat bread and wine and special words to remember that God rescued the Jews from slavery in Egypt. This year's Passover meal is different, though. Jesus takes the bread *(hold it up)*, thanks God for it *(look up to heaven)*, blesses it *(put hands over it)*, breaks it *(break it)* and gives it to his friends *(break off bits to give each child, if they want it, but they don't have to eat it)*.

Then Jesus says some new words. I wonder what he says . . . *('This is my body, given for you')*. Jesus does the same with the wine *(hold up cup)*. He thanks God for it *(look up to heaven)*, blesses it *(put hands over it)* and gives it to his friends. Jesus passes round one cup for his friends to share, but I'm going to pour some drink into these cups to give you if you want it - it's not wine, only juice, and you don't have to drink it. *(Extra helper washes up cups between groups.)*

Again, Jesus says some new words. I wonder what he says . . . *('This is my blood, shed for you.')* I wonder how the disciples feel . . . *(Maybe puzzled, surprised, shocked.)* I wonder what Jesus means . . . *(Jesus is helping his friends understand what's going to happen, that he will die on the cross the next day, Good Friday. We know this, but his friends don't know before it happens. Jesus wants his friends to remember him, to remember his teaching about loving, forgiving and sharing, so we can carry on his work and help other people know God and know how to live in God's world.)*

Jesus says, 'Do this to remember me.' We were remembering Jesus as we went through the Last Supper just now. Christians remember the Last Supper in church in a special service called . . . ? *(Mass, the Eucharist, Holy Communion, the Lord's Supper - different churches have different names for it.)*

(Point out the altar/table, bread and wine.) The priest or minister thanks God, blesses and shares the bread and wine with the people in church, just as Jesus does with his friends.

Extra for Years 5 and 6 if needed

I wonder if you have bread and wine in church . . . I wonder what it means to you . . .

When Christians share bread and wine in church, we believe that Jesus is with us, just as he was with his friends at the Last Supper. We believe that Jesus helps us be like him - more loving and forgiving, sharing with and helping others. We believe Jesus rescues us from our sins, our selfishness and self-centredness.

Helper **Activity 1**

Let's be quiet for a moment to think about the people we love and people who love us. If you want, you can thank God for your family and friends. You can thank God for loving each of us too.

Helper **Activity 2**

Here is the word 'Love' to put in your group's envelope to take to the next activity when the buzzer or bell sounds.

Helper **Activity 3**

Make a cup and plate for your Easter garden *(show the ready-made examples)*. Fold a square of foil in half, matching the corners so you make a rectangle. Wrap the top half around your finger, then twist it in the middle and flatten the bottom end to make the foot for your chalice. Fold the edges of the other square of foil under, then tilt them up to make the edges of a small square plate. Add these to your garden with the small dots of Blu-Tack. Is there anything you want to say or ask about the story? We may not have the answers, but we'll note down your questions. Some things about God are hard to understand.

Group 3: The cross – forgiveness (10 minutes)

Helpers should read the story beforehand in Luke 23.

Materials required Pens, labels, polystyrene dishes, straws, scissors, sticky tape, hot cross buns, eight photocopies of the scripts for the play on card or in plastic wallets, eight baseball hats – labelled 'Jesus', 'Priest', 'Thief 1' and 'Thief 2' and four marked 'Crowd' (optional), large picture of Good Friday, printed word 'Forgiveness'.

Visual focus Large picture of Good Friday, hot cross buns and printed word 'Forgiveness'.

With the first group, make a name badge – just their first name, written clearly – and write their full name on a dish.

Remember to keep ideas simple for Years 3 and 4, but expect more discussion with Years 5 and 6.

Helper *(Show hot cross buns.)* I wonder why we have hot cross buns . . . *(Remind us that Jesus dies on the cross on Good Friday.)*

We're going to look at the story now. *(Hand out the eight labelled baseball hats, if using, and scripts for the Good Friday play. See page 66.)*

Helper **Activity 1**

Here is the word 'Forgiveness' to put in your group's envelope to take to the next activity when the buzzer or bell sounds.

Helper **Activity 2**

Make a cross for your Easter garden. Cut a straw across two-thirds along its length, then stick the short piece across the long piece to form a cross shape. I wonder what you think about Good Friday . . .

Helper **Activity 3**

Jesus forgives the people who hurt him on the cross. He wants us to forgive people who hurt us too. Let's be quiet for a little while and think about anyone we need to

Good Friday play – Jesus dies on the cross

(You will need a narrator (an adult), Priest, Pilate, Jesus, Thief 1, Thief 2 and the Crowd.)

Narrator The priests want to get rid of Jesus but only Pilate, the Roman governor, can order Jesus' death. The guards take Jesus to Pilate.

Priest This man Jesus is making trouble. He says he's the king of the Jews.

Narrator Pilate speaks to Jesus but can't find anything wrong. The crowd shout:

Crowd Crucify, crucify him!

Pilate Jesus has done no wrong.

Crowd Crucify, crucify him!

Pilate It's the Passover festival so I shall set one prisoner free. Let me free Jesus.

Crowd Crucify, crucify him!

Narrator Pilate hands Jesus to the soldiers. They beat Jesus, mock him and make him carry a heavy cross to Golgotha, the Place of the Skull. Two thieves are crucified with Jesus, who is put in between them. The soldiers play a game of dice as they wait for the prisoners to die.

Jesus Father, forgive them. They don't know what they're doing.

Priest You saved other people. Save yourself, if you are God's chosen king.

Thief 1 Yes. Why don't you save us all?

Thief 2 Be quiet. Jesus is a good man. Jesus, remember me when you come into your kingdom.

Jesus Don't worry. Today you will be with me in heaven.

Narrator Jesus suffered until 3 p.m. He died with a loud cry.

Jesus Father, I give you my spirit.

Narrator Jesus dies. The soldiers thrust a spear into his side to make sure. His friends take Jesus down from the cross and put him in a tomb. Everyone thinks this is the end of Jesus.

RE Active Church (London: SPCK). Copyright © Jenny Gray 2012

forgive . . . anything we are sorry for saying or doing or forgetting to do. If we want to, we can say sorry to God and know he forgives us. Is there anything you want to say or ask about the story? We may not have the answers, but we'll note down your questions. Some things about God are hard to understand.

Group 4: The Resurrection – new life (10 minutes)

Helpers should read the story beforehand in John 20.1-20.

Materials required   Pens, labels, polystyrene dishes, large picture of Easter Day, green soft modelling dough, 30 small stones, 30 flowers to colour, 30 cocktail sticks, sticky tape, bulb, pot, pot of flowers, Easter cards, printed words 'New life'.

Visual focus   Large picture of Easter Day, pot of flowers, printed words 'New life'.

With the first group, make a name badge – just their first name, written clearly – and write their full name on a dish.

Remember to keep ideas simple for Years 3 and 4, but expect more discussion with Years 5 and 6.

Helper   Easter is in the spring. Spring is full of new life. I wonder if you can think of some examples . . . *(Lambs, chicks, bees buzzing round flowers, butterflies, spring flowers.)*

Have you ever planted seeds or bulbs and watched them grow? I wonder what happens . . . *(Hold up the bulb and pot.)* You put bulbs or seeds in the ground or in a pot, they look dead, but you cover them with earth. You wait, you water the earth, then green shoots and flowers appear. The bulbs or seeds really are alive.

Seeds and flowers help us understand what happens to Jesus at Easter. I wonder if you know what happens on Easter Day . . . *(Use the children's Easter gardens to reinforce the story.)* Jesus dies on the cross on Good Friday, on a hill outside Jerusalem. *(Mould a small hill out of a piece of the green soft modelling dough to go in one of the Easter gardens.)*

His friends put his body in a tomb, like a cave, in the garden *(Make a hole in the green hill)*.

They close the tomb with a round stone *(add stone)*. Everyone thinks that is the end of Jesus but, three days later, on Easter Day, the stone is rolled away *(move stone aside)* and the tomb is empty *(show inside)*.

God gives Jesus new life. His friends meet Jesus again. It's hard to believe, but they can see Jesus is alive. The flower you are going to add to your garden is a sign of Jesus' new life *(stick a flower on a cocktail stick into the green hill)*. The flower reminds us that Jesus' death is not the end. Easter Day follows Good Friday. Christians believe that God gives new life to Jesus and gives us new life when we die.

There's even more to celebrate. Christians believe that God gives us new life here on earth. God plants seeds of love in us and helps us to be like Jesus. Jesus is full of God's love, always helping others. Being a Christian means being like Jesus Christ, being Christ-like, helping others too. I wonder what you think about this . . .

Flowers are a sign of new life, which is why there are often flowers on Easter cards *(show)*, as well as the other signs of new life we talked about – chicks, butterflies, lambs and so on.

Helper   **Activity 1**

Here are the words 'New life' to put in your group's envelope to take to the next activity when the buzzer or bell sounds.

Helper

Activity 2

Make a tomb for your garden from a small piece of the green soft modelling dough, then add a stone to the side of the entrance. Colour a flower, put it on a cocktail stick and add it to your garden. Is there anything you want to say or ask about the story? We may not have the answers, but we'll note down your questions. Some things about God are hard to understand.

Extra for Years 5 and 6 if needed

I wonder how people would describe you . . . Are you like Jesus . . . ? Are you kind or unkind, happy or grumpy, generous or greedy, helpful or unhelpful . . . ? Don't worry, you don't have to say anything out loud, unless you want to! I wonder what kind of person you would like to be . . .

Workshop 3: Easter friends

Overview of workshop See the at-a-glance summary, page 117.

You will need
- Timer.
- CD player.
- CD of Easter or general songs, plus words and music (for example, 'The Best Worship Songs . . . Ever' boxed sets, traditional hymns, Handel's *Messiah*, other oratorios, Out of the Ark Music[4]), plus optional song, *Friends* theme tune,[5] 'When I needed a neighbour', 'He'll be there'[6] or 'Jesus is a friend of mine'[7] or other.

For each class of 30: felt-tip pens, sticky labels, hot cross bun cards to colour, mini chocolate eggs, pictures of Palm Sunday and Jesus' arrest and trial and the Last Supper, Taizé cross, the Resurrection with Mary Magdalene and/or Thomas with Jesus (Turvey[8] or others), a coconut (halved and cleaned), any cross.

For Group 2: knitted or toy figures to represent the Last Supper or large picture, bread and wafers, wine in a chalice or small cups, children's and adults' Bibles.

For Group 3: 30 strands of wool 20–30 cm long, home-made trellis cross[9] (also used in 'Jesus changes lives' workshop, Chapter 7).

For Group 4: a relighting candle.

Preparation Play the CD of songs as the children come in and leave. Set up four small-group areas, with the visual focus as indicated in the materials for each group (see below). Photocopy the notes for the helpers and gather together all the other materials required.

Craft The children colour the A5 hot cross bun cards (see template, Chapter 10). On the back is a Bible text and invitation to church activities. There is space to include the address of the church website (and joint town churches' website), if available, to help parents and children follow up the experience in church.

Leader

Introduction to each class (5 minutes)

(Welcome the children at the church door and lead them to the pews or seats at the front of the church. Invite them to put their coats and so on under the pews or seats to be collected at the end of the session.)

Welcome to our 'Easter friends' workshop. I wonder what makes a good friend . . . *(Someone you like to be with, talk with, listen to, share with, you help each other.)*

Christians think God is our good friend. We spend time with God, when we pray and read the Bible and come to church, because we know God cares for us and helps us. Jesus shows us what God is like, so today we're going to find out about Jesus and his friends.

Your teacher will put you into four small groups to go round each activity. The buzzer will tell us when to change.

We'll give you a sticky label to write your name on, so we know who you are – just your first name as clearly as you can. The team members have their labels on already – let me introduce them to you now . . . You will also be given a hot cross bun Easter card to colour *(show)*. There are four different parts of the Easter story to work on, based on our Easter friends theme. We hope you'll show people at home your card and tell them what you did in church today.

Leader   **Conclusion to each session (15 minutes)**

Hold up your cards – they look good! If you haven't finished them, perhaps you can finish them at school or at home. Let's go through the Easter story together to put it in order. I'll use this coconut *(hold halves of coconut)* to prompt you. Put up your hands to tell me . . . *(make clip, clop noise as you tap the coconut halves together for the donkey)*, Palm Sunday . . . *(hold up one half for wine)*, Maundy Thursday *(hold one half upside down for the hill where the crosses are)*, Good Friday *(notice the marks on the coconut half for the three crosses)* and *(show the coconut half, open side facing the children, like the empty tomb on)* Easter Day.

Christians are friends of Jesus Christ and we want to be like him. *(Hold up the cross.)* I wonder if any of you wear a cross . . . ? The cross reminds us of Jesus, how he lived and died and rose again for us. Jesus always thinks about God and other people, just as the cross points up to God *(point up)* and out to other people *(point outwards)*. Christians try to do this too. We believe that God helps us in good times and in bad, and we try to help other people as well.

The songs we have been hearing remind us that God is always with us to help us, and God wants us to help others. You can join in as we listen to the theme tune from *Friends* – 'I'll be there for you' *(or other optional song, if using)*. Then we can sing a song you know from school *(verses of 'When I needed a neighbour', 'Jesus is a friend of mine, 'He'll be there' or other, if using)*.

(Ask helpers for any interesting questions or comments.)

Thank you for working so well today. We'll leave the trellis cross with your wool prayers in church so the congregation can see on Sunday what you have been doing with us. Enjoy your little chocolate egg when your teacher says you can eat it. Don't forget your invitation to *(mention any special services or events here, as appropriate)*. A happy Easter to you all.

Group 1: Going with the crowd (10 minutes)

Helpers should read the story beforehand in John 12.12–19 and, for Good Friday, John 19.4–16.

Materials required   Pens, labels, hot cross bun cards to colour, large pictures of Palm Sunday and Jesus' arrest or trial (Turvey or other).

Visual focus   Large pictures of Palm Sunday and Jesus' arrest or trial.

With the first group, make a name badge – just their first name, written clearly – and write their full name on a card.

Remember to keep ideas simple for Years 3 and 4, but expect more discussion with Years 5 and 6.

Helper   I wonder if you've ever been in a big crowd – maybe at a football or rugby match, a concert or other event . . . Cheering crowds can be exciting and fun, but sometimes crowds are scary and dangerous. Maybe you've seen crowds rioting on TV . . .

I wonder if you would join in with others in the crowd. Listen to these questions and possible answers in our Friends' Quiz and think whether you would do answers (a), (b) or (c).

Two boys or girls are fighting in the playground. Do you:

(a) find an adult to stop it

(b) join the crowd shouting 'fight, fight, fight'

(c) pretend you didn't see anything?

Your friends are meeting up on Sunday, when you visit your family or go to church. You're worried your friends might laugh. Do you:

(a) tell them the truth

(b) nag your mum into letting you go

(c) tell them you'll come and not turn up?

Your friend turns up with sweets *(or alcohol for Years 5 and 6)*, saying that he or she has taken them from the cupboard at home. Do you:

(a) refuse the sweets *(or alcohol)*

(b) take some sweets *(or alcohol)* from your own cupboard to add to the feast

(c) eat the sweets *(drink the alcohol)*, but feel guilty?

If you decided on mostly (a)s – well done, you stand up for what you believe and don't just go with the crowd.

If you decided on mostly (b)s – you go with the crowd even if it's wrong. You need to think for yourself.

If you decided on mostly (c)s – you don't stand up for what you believe and end up feeling bad about yourself.

(Show the Palm Sunday picture.) I wonder what's happening in the pictures . . . I wonder what you know about the story of Palm Sunday . . . *(Include the crowd shouting 'Hosanna' as Jesus rides into Jerusalem on a donkey, the crowd welcomes Jesus as the Messiah, God's special king who will rescue the Jews from their enemies and make them a great nation, a superpower, Jesus is thought of as their leader, a hero, the crowd lays down coats and palm branches for the donkey to walk on, like rolling out a red carpet, but then, just a few days later, on Good Friday, the crowd in Jerusalem treats Jesus very differently.)*

(Show the picture of Jesus' arrest.) I wonder what you can see . . . I wonder what you know about Good Friday . . . *(Include the soldiers arresting Jesus and taking him to the priests, who want to kill him because they don't believe he's God's Son, but the priests, as they don't have the power to kill Jesus, take him to the Roman governor, Pilate. Pilate can't find anything that Jesus has done wrong and he wants to release him, but the crowd shouts, 'Crucify him!' It was Passover, a special Jewish festival, so Pilate offers to free a prisoner – he hopes they'll choose Jesus, but the crowd chooses Barabbas, a criminal. Pilate knows it's wrong to kill Jesus, but he*

doesn't stand up to the crowd. Instead, he takes a bowl of water and washes his hands of the affair.)

I wonder how you'd feel if you were in the crowd shouting 'Hosanna!' . . . Would you join in?

I wonder how you'd feel if you were in the crowd shouting 'Crucify him!' . . . Would you join in?

Is it easier to go with the crowd or stand up to a crowd?

Extra for Years 5 and 6 if needed

I wonder why Pilate lets Jesus die . . . Remember, there are no wrong answers, just say what you think. *(Fears a riot, he'll lose control, lose his job.)*

I wonder why the crowd shouts 'Crucify him!' . . . *(The priests have supporters in the crowd, people are frightened to stand up to them, they're disappointed that Jesus is not the fighting king they had expected.)*

At Easter, some churches read the story aloud and everyone has to shout 'Crucify him!' I wonder how you'd feel about doing this . . .

Helper

Activity

Colour the 'Going with the crowd' part of the hot cross bun card (numbered 1). Is there anything you want to say or ask about the story? We may not have the answers, but we'll note down your questions. Some things about God are hard to understand.

Group 2: A meal to remember (10 minutes)

Helpers should read the story beforehand in Luke 22.14-20 and 1 Corinthians 11.23-25.

Materials required   Pens, labels, hot cross bun cards to colour, knitted or toy figures to represent the Last Supper or large picture, bread and wafers, wine in a chalice or small cups, children's and adults' Bibles.

Visual focus   Knitted or toy figures to represent the Last Supper or large picture.

With the first group, make a name badge – just their first name, written clearly – and write their full name on a card.

Remember to keep ideas simple for Years 3 and 4, but expect more discussion with Years 5 and 6.

Helper   I wonder how you remember things . . . *(Diary, phone or electronic organizer, lists, sticky notes, ask someone to remind you, say it over and over.)*

(Unpack Last Supper figures and let the children arrange them to create the scene, or look at the Last Supper picture.)

I wonder which one is Jesus . . . *(He's usually in white, which is a sign of holiness.)*

Not everyone around the table is Jesus' friend. One of them is Judas, who betrays Jesus. I wonder which one is Judas . . . It's a tricky question as you can't tell from the outside what people are like on the inside. Only God knows what we're like on the inside.

I wonder what you know about the Last Supper . . . *(Piece together the story. Jesus knows he's going to die, he wants his friends to remember him. The night before he dies, Jesus shares the Jewish Passover meal with his friends, as Jews do every year to remember their ancestors' escape from slavery in Egypt. They have the bread and wine, but Jesus adds surprising new words . . . 'This is my body, broken for you' and 'This is my blood, shed for you'.)*

I wonder how the disciples feel when they hear Jesus' words . . . ? *(Shocked, puzzled, surprised, worried, sad.)*

I wonder what you think about his words . . . *(It's OK to be puzzled or shocked.)*

I wonder what Jesus wants to tell us . . . *(Jesus wants his friends to know he's going to die because they don't know this is going to happen. Jesus is giving his life for us because he loves us.)* Jesus' words aren't easy to understand, so different churches have different ideas about what Jesus means.

Extra for Years 5 and 6 if needed

Here are some ideas about Jesus' death.

- It's God's plan to rescue the world from all that's wrong and spoils us.
- Jesus is a sacrifice, 'the lamb of God which takes away the sins of the world'.
- Jesus pays the penalty for the things we do wrong, (our sins), to make us friends with God.
- Jesus gives us an example to follow: 'No one has greater love than this, to lay down one's life for one's friends.'

I wonder what you think of these ideas.

Jesus says, 'Do this to remember me', so Christians share the Last Supper in church in a service called Holy Communion or the Eucharist or Mass or the Lord's Supper – different churches have different names. *(Show the bread and wafers.)* In the service, the priest or minister tells the story and gives the people bread, real bread or wafer bread like this, with the words 'The body of Christ'. *(Show the chalice or small cups.)* The priest gives the people wine with the words 'The blood of Christ'. I wonder if any of you have seen bread and wine in church . . .

We remember Jesus by sharing the Last Supper in church with bread and wine and the words Jesus gave us. I wonder if other things help us remember Jesus too . . . *(Prompt if needed and show the different Bibles for adults and children.)* We remember Jesus by reading the stories about him in the Bible, aloud in church or at home.

Matthew, Mark, Luke and John wrote down the stories about him to help us remember. I wonder if you have a Bible at home or at school . . .

I wonder if you read any of the stories at home or at school . . .

I wonder what's your favourite Bible story . . .

Helper　　**Activity**

Colour the 'A meal to remember' part of the hot cross bun card (numbered 2). Is there anything you want to say or ask about the story? We may not have the answers, but we'll note down your questions. Some things about God are hard to understand.

Group 3: I'll be there for you (10 minutes)

Helpers should read the story beforehand in John 19.16–19 and 25–30.

Materials required　　Pens, labels, hot cross bun cards to colour, *Friends* theme tune, 30 strands of wool 20–30 cm long, home-made trellis cross, picture of Taizé cross.

Visual focus	Picture of Taizé cross.

With the first group, make a name badge – just their first name, written clearly – and write their full name on a card.

Remember to keep ideas simple for Years 3 and 4, but expect more discussion with Years 5 and 6.

Helper

(Listen to Friends *theme tune. Think about the words together – you may like to write them out beforehand.)* I wonder what the *Friends* theme tune is about . . . *(Friends being there for each other.)*

(Show picture of the Taizé cross.) I wonder who these two people are . . . *(John and Mary. Piece together the story of Jesus' death: when Jesus was crucified, his disciples ran away, but one stayed with him to the end and his name was John.)*

John must have been a very special person to stay with Jesus as he suffered. Of course, there is someone who stays with us always and sees us through bad times. I wonder who this is . . . *(The children may say God or their mother.)* We can't see God but he is always with us.

Jesus' mother, Mary, also stays with Jesus at the foot of the cross. Jesus is in great pain, but he still thinks about other people. Jesus tells Mary to look after his friend John as if he were her son. He also tells John to take care of his mother as if she were his own mother. I wonder why Jesus does this . . . Say what you think . . . remember, there are no wrong answers.

I wonder if it's better to have someone with you or be on your own if you are sad or sick . . . Mary and John can't stop Jesus hurting and dying on the cross, but they don't want him to suffer on his own. They stay with him to show he matters to them. We can't always stop people hurting, but we can be there with them. Being with people makes a difference – it's less scary, it shows they matter, it shows we care. I wonder if you have any examples of this . . .

People from church visit those who are sick in hospital or at home. Christians believe prayer helps people too. We ask God to help people, to give them comfort and strength. Many people tell us they are helped by prayer.

Helper

Activity 1

I wonder if you can think of people in trouble, who need help – people in the news or friends and family. If you like, you can tie a piece of wool on to our cross as you remember them and you can quietly ask God to help them. We will leave the cross in church with the words 'I'll be there for you' and a note to explain.

Helper

Activity 2

Colour the 'I'll be there for you' part of the hot cross bun card (numbered 3). Is there anything you want to say or ask? We may not have the answers but we'll note down your questions. Some things about God are hard to understand.

Group 4: A friend for ever (10 minutes)

Helpers should read the story beforehand in John 20.1-18 and 24-29.

Materials required Pens, labels, hot cross bun cards to colour, relighting candle, large pictures of the Resurrection with Mary Magdalene and/or Thomas with Jesus.

Visual focus

Large pictures of the Resurrection with Mary Magdalene and/or Thomas with Jesus.

With the first group, make a name badge - just their first name, written clearly - and write their full name on a card.

Remember to keep ideas simple for Years 3 and 4, but expect more discussion with Years 5 and 6.

Helper

I wonder how you'd feel if a friend or relative moved away . . . (Maybe sad, lonely, you miss them, angry they've gone, you might forget them or find it hard to keep in touch.)

I wonder how you could keep in touch . . . (Phone, text, email, Skype, letters, cards, visits.)

I wonder how often you'd keep in touch . . . (Maybe every day, week, month, once a year at Christmas, depends how special they are.)

I wonder how Jesus' friends feel when he's taken away and put to death on the cross . . . (Sad, frightened, lonely, surprised, shocked, angry, empty, they hide together in the Upper Room where they had the Last Supper.)

Good Friday is not the end of Jesus though. Jesus dies on the cross, but God gives him new life. Jesus is dead (light and blow out the relighting candle), but he defeats death and rises to new life, like this candle flame that can't be put out. After Easter, Jesus meets his friends again - until he goes to be with God in heaven 50 days later, on Ascension Day.

I wonder if you know any stories about Jesus meeting his friends after Easter . . . (Choose either Mary or Thomas or both if you have time.)

(Show a picture of Mary Magdalene meeting Jesus.) I wonder what you can see . . .

I wonder if you know what happens on Easter morning . . . (Piece together the story: Mary loves Jesus very much and, on Easter morning, she goes to the tomb in the garden where Jesus is buried to anoint his body with expensive perfumes, like myrrh. She finds the stone rolled away and the tomb empty. An angel tells her that Jesus is alive. Mary meets Jesus in the garden, but she thinks he's the gardener. Her eyes are blurred with tears and Jesus is somehow different. Jesus calls Mary by her name and it is then that Mary knows it really is Jesus.)

I wonder how Mary feels now . . . (Surprised, happy, puzzled, brave, because her friend Jesus really is alive.)

The other disciples meet Jesus too. I wonder if you know the story of doubting Thomas . . . (Piece together the story: Jesus comes into the room where his friends the disciples are hiding. They see for themselves that Jesus is alive, just as Mary told them, but one disciple, called Thomas, is not there. When he arrives and Jesus has gone, Thomas refuses to believe that Jesus is alive. He wants to see Jesus for himself and touch the marks the nails and spear made in Jesus' hands and side. Thomas stays with his friends and, when Jesus comes into the room again, he sees for himself that Jesus really is alive and doubts no longer.) I wonder how you feel about that story . . .

Extra for Years 5 and 6 if needed

When Jesus goes to heaven, he promises the disciples that a new friend will come - the Holy Spirit. When Jesus was alive on earth, he could only be in one time and place, but the coming of the Holy Spirit means Jesus is with us always, everywhere. We cannot see him, but we know he is our friend for ever.

Helper	Activity

Colour the 'A friend for ever' part of the hot cross bun card (numbered 4). Is there anything you want to say or ask? We may not have the answers but we'll note down your questions. Some things about God are hard to understand.

Workshop 4: Eggy Easter

Overview of workshop   See the at-a-glance summary, page 117.

You will need
- Timer.
- CD player.
- CD of Easter or general songs, plus words and music (for example, 'The Best Worship Songs . . . Ever' boxed sets, traditional hymns, Handel's *Messiah*, other oratorios, Out of the Ark Music), plus optional song 'Lord, I lift your name on high'.[10]

For each class of 30: felt-tip pens, sticky labels, Easter egg cards to colour, sticky notes, large pictures of Palm Sunday, Good Friday and Easter Day (Neil Thorogood's[11] or other), a big chocolate Easter egg, Easter decorations, such as a 'Happy Easter' banner (optional), Easter tree,[12] Easter cards, four small tables, each with six plastic eggs in an egg box, each egg filled with one item as indicated for each group below, mini chocolate eggs.

Extra for Years 5 and 6 if needed

Four large pieces of card with the headings 'Palm Sunday', 'Maundy Thursday', 'Good Friday' and 'Easter Day' for sticky notes headlines.

For Group 1: the plastic eggs to contain a small toy donkey, small palm leaf (drawn or real), piece of cloth, word 'Hosanna', small building bricks forming a wall (for Jerusalem), scroll (made from a cocktail stick and paper) with the word 'Zechariah' on it; plus a palm cross.

For Group 2: the plastic eggs to contain a small piece of bread, small chalice (can be made from silver foil), Judas' coins (small silver coins), X (for kiss), words 'Remember me' and rope noose; plus Communion bread and wine, small whiteboard and cloth.

For Group 3: the plastic eggs to contain small nails, cross or crucifix, spear, crown of thorns, dice and word 'Forgive'; plus eight large nails (you may need to file the tips so they are not sharp).

For Group 4: five of the plastic eggs to contain a piece of white cloth, small round stone, angel, chocolate egg and word 'Joy' (leaving one egg empty); plus photocopies of scripts for play in plastic wallets or on card, tomb made from two chairs covered with a sheet or blanket and a large piece of card cut out for the stone.

Preparation   Play the CD as the children come in and leave. Set up four small-group areas, with the visual focus as indicated in the materials for each group (below). Photocopy the notes for the helpers and gather together all the other materials required.

Craft   The children colour the Easter egg cards (see template, Chapter 10). On the back there is a Bible text and invitation to church activities. You may include the address of the church website (and joint town churches' website), if available, to help parents and children follow up the experience in church.

Leader

Introduction to each class (5 minutes)

(Welcome the children at the church door and lead them to the pews or seats at the front of the church. Invite them to put their coats and so on under the pews or seats to be collected at the end of the session.)

Welcome to our 'Eggy Easter' workshop. We've planned an 'eggciting' session for you today, with mystery eggs for you to open to help you think about Easter.

Your teacher will put you into four small groups to go round each activity. The buzzer will tell us when to change.

We'll give you a sticky label to write your name on, so we know who you are – just your first name as clearly as you can. The team members have their labels on already – let me introduce them to you now . . . You will also be given a special Easter egg card *(show)*. We hope you'll show people at home your 'eggy' card and tell them what you did in church today.

Leader

Conclusion to each session (15 minutes)

A lot happens in the week before Easter – the week we call Holy Week. All the stories we've looked at today happen in this one week. Let's put the days in the right order using our pictures . . . hands up to tell me.

Extra for Years 5 and 6 if needed

(Collect the four cards with the sticky notes headlines from the small groups.) We'll read out the headlines on your sticky notes on our four cards headed 'Palm Sunday', 'Maundy Thursday', 'Good Friday' and 'Easter Day' . . . We'll leave them as a display in church, along with the eggs and egg boxes, so the congregation can see on Sunday what you have been doing with us.

I wonder what you think is a very important time of year for Christians? Hands up for Christmas . . . hands up for Easter . . .

Christians believe Easter is very important. We celebrate Jesus' birth at Christmas, but Jesus dies and rises to new life at Easter. Easter means new life for Jesus and for us.

We celebrate in church with joyful hymns and songs. We have lots of flowers, which are special because we don't have flowers in church now during Lent when we are getting ready for Easter.

We celebrate at home with Easter cards, chocolate eggs, maybe make an Easter tree or Easter banners *(show)*. We're going to celebrate with you by giving you a little chocolate egg and teaching you an action song about Jesus – the chorus to 'Lord, I lift your name on high'[13] *(play CD if there isn't a confident singer in your team)*. I'll go through the words and actions first, then you can all join in.

> heaven *(lift both arms up)*
> earth *(both arms down)*
> show *(arms out in front, palms up)*,
> earth *(arms back down low)*
> cross *(stretch arms out wide)*
> pay *(arms in front, one hand on the other, which is palm up)*;
> cross *(stretch arms out wide)*
> grave *(both hands down low)*,

sky *(lift arms up high)*,
I lift *(wave arms high)*.
(Bring both hands down again and repeat.)

(Ask helpers for any interesting questions or comments.)

Thank you for working so well today. We'll display the Years 5 and 6 newspaper headlines and our eggs in the egg boxes in church so the congregation can see on Sunday what you have been doing with us. Enjoy your little egg when your teacher says you can eat it. Don't forget your invitation to *(mention any special services or events here, as appropriate)*. A happy Easter to you all.

Group 1: Hosanna (10 minutes)

Helpers should read the story beforehand in Mark 11.1–11.

Materials required   Pens, labels, Easter egg cards to colour, sticky notes, large picture of Palm Sunday, small table, six plastic eggs in an egg box filled with a small toy donkey, small palm leaf (drawn or real), piece of cloth, word 'Hosanna', small building bricks forming a wall (for Jerusalem), scroll (made from a cocktail stick and paper) with the word 'Zechariah' on it; plus a palm cross.

Extra for Years 5 and 6 if needed

Large piece of card with the headings 'Palm Sunday' for sticky notes headline.

Visual focus   Small table with large picture of Palm Sunday and egg box with the filled plastic eggs.

With the first group, make a name badge – just their first name, written clearly – and write their full name on a card.

Remember to keep ideas simple for Years 3 and 4, but expect more discussion with Years 5 and 6.

Helper   *(Let the children open the filled plastic eggs and say what they know about Palm Sunday, adding any bits they leave out or don't know, to explain the contents of the eggs. Include that the prophet Zechariah told the Jews their king would come to Jerusalem riding on a donkey, so the people are excited and cheer Jesus as their special king. They shout 'Hosanna', wave palm leaves and put their coats on the ground. They think Jesus will drive out the Roman rulers and make Israel the top nation. **Important**: Put the eggs back in the box for the next group.)*

(Show the large Palm Sunday picture.) I wonder what you can see . . . I wonder how it makes you feel . . . Remember, there are no wrong answers – just say what you think.

Where is Jesus in the picture? What is he like?

Jesus isn't the king people expect and he's not like other kings. Jesus doesn't stand out from the crowd on his donkey. A donkey's not like the warhorses the Romans rode in their parades; a donkey is a sign of peace, not power. Let's check out what Jesus is like.

- Does Jesus have an army to fight the Romans? *(No, Jesus comes in peace.)*
- Does Jesus have lots of money? *(No, Jesus is happy to be poor.)*

- Does Jesus have a crown and fine clothes? *(No, Jesus is ordinary, like us.)*
- Does Jesus have servants to wait on him? *(No, Jesus comes to serve us, to help us know God and live in God's way.)*

I wonder what kind of king you think is best – one who looks after his people or after his own interests? One who fights wars or loves his enemies?

Helper   **Activity 1**

Colour the donkey and 'Hosanna!' on the Easter egg card.

Helper   **Activity 2 (Years 3 and 4)**

Have you been part of a cheering crowd . . . at a sports event, concert, elsewhere . . . ? Did you cheer? If so, why? How did you feel?

The crowd shouts 'Hosanna', praise to Jesus. Christians all over the world praise Jesus today in songs, hymns and prayers. Many churches have palm crosses on Palm Sunday *(show)*. Christians keep them at home afterwards to remind us of the story and to remind us to be like Jesus.

Helper   **Activity 2 (Years 5 and 6)**

Imagine you are reporters for the *Jerusalem Herald* newspaper. Decide, as a group, on a headline for your newspaper for Palm Sunday. Write it down on a sticky note and stick it to the large piece of card with the heading 'Palm Sunday' on it. These will be shared at the end of the workshop and make a display to leave in church.

(For all years.) Is there anything you want to say or ask about the story? We may not have the answers, but we'll note down your questions. Some things about God are hard to understand.

Group 2: Remember me (10 minutes)

Helpers should read the story beforehand in Matthew 26.26–30.

Materials required   Pens, labels, Easter egg cards to colour, six plastic eggs in an egg box filled with a small piece of bread, small chalice (can be made from silver foil), Judas' coins (small silver coins), X (for kiss), words 'Remember me' and rope noose; plus Communion bread and wine, small whiteboard and cloth.

Extra for Years 5 and 6 if needed

Large piece of card with the heading 'Maundy Thursday' for sticky notes headlines.

Visual focus   Small table with Communion bread and wine and egg box with the filled plastic eggs.

With the first group, make a name badge – just their first name, written clearly – and write their full name on a card.

Remember to keep ideas simple for Years 3 and 4, but expect more discussion with Years 5 and 6.

Helper   *(Let the children open the plastic eggs and say what they know about the Last Supper, adding any bits they leave out or don't know, to explain the contents of the eggs. Include that Jesus shares a special meal with his friends before he dies, called the Last Supper, and says special words over the bread and wine – 'This is my body', 'This is my blood',*

'Do this to remember me'. One of Jesus' friends, Judas, turns against Jesus. The Jewish High Priest gives Judas 30 pieces of silver to betray Jesus. Judas leads the guards to Jesus in the Garden of Gethsemane and identifies him with a kiss, then Jesus is arrested and taken away to be crucified. Judas is sorry - he feels bad about betraying his friend, so he tries to give back the 30 pieces of silver, then he hangs himself with a rope noose.
Important*: Put the eggs back in the box for the next group.)*

I wonder why Judas betrays Jesus . . . Remember, there are no wrong answers, just say what you think . . . *(Maybe Judas is greedy - 30 pieces of silver was a lot of money - or maybe Judas wants Jesus to be a different kind of king who will fight the Romans and make his disciples rich and powerful.)*

Judas is sorry for what he's done. I wonder if Jesus forgives Judas . . . *(Christians believe that Jesus forgives everyone who is sorry. Everyone gets things wrong sometimes. Can anyone honestly say that they never say or do anything nasty, that they always try to help other people?)*

Sometimes we say or do things that we know are wrong. Sometimes we can't be bothered to help other people. You don't have to say anything, but would anyone like to give an example . . . ? *(You could give some examples, such as not helping with jobs at home when asked, being rude to a parent or teacher, being mean to a sister, brother, friend or pet, not sharing.)*

When we've done wrong, we feel bad, but we can say sorry and know God forgives us. God wipes the slate clean and gives us a fresh start - a bit like wiping writing off a whiteboard *(show)*.

I wonder if we have to be in church to say sorry to God . . . *(No - we can say sorry to God wherever we are. We know God forgives us if we are truly sorry.)*

(Show the bread and chalice laid out on the table.) I wonder what happens here . . . *(Service in church called the Eucharist or Holy Communion or Mass or the Lord's Supper. The priest or minister gives the people bread and wine. We remember the Last Supper, we remember that Jesus forgives us and helps us be like him.)* I wonder if you receive bread and wine in your church . . .

Helper   **Activity**

Colour the bread and wine and 'Remember me' on the Easter egg card.

Helper   **Activity (Years 5 and 6)**

Imagine you are reporters for the *Jerusalem Herald* newspaper. Decide, as a group, on a headline for your newspaper for Maundy Thursday. Write it down on a sticky note and stick it to the large piece of card with the heading 'Maundy Thursday' on it. These will be shared at the end of the workshop and make a display to leave in church.

(For all years.) Is there anything you want to say or ask about the story? We may not have the answers, but we'll note down your questions. Some things about God are hard to understand.

Group 3: Father forgive (10 minutes)

Helpers should read the story beforehand in Luke 23.26-43.

Materials required   Pens, labels, Easter egg cards to colour, sticky notes, large picture of Good Friday, six plastic eggs in an egg box filled with small nails, cross or crucifix, spear, crown of thorns, dice and word 'Forgive'; plus eight large nails (you may need to file the tips so they are not sharp).

Extra for Years 5 and 6 if needed

Large piece of card with the heading 'Good Friday' for sticky notes headlines.

Visual focus

Small table with large picture of Good Friday, cross or crucifix and egg box with the filled plastic eggs.

With the first group, make a name badge - just their first name, written clearly - and write their full name on a card.

Remember to keep ideas simple for Years 3 and 4, but expect more discussion with Years 5 and 6.

Helper

*(Let the children open the plastic eggs and say what they know about Good Friday, adding any bits they leave out or don't know, to explain the contents of the eggs. Include that Joseph, Jesus' father, was a carpenter and Jesus was a carpenter too. He used nails and wood to make good things, so it's sad to see wood and nails used to kill him on the cross. Soldiers put a crown of thorns on Jesus' head, they play dice as they wait for Jesus to die and they check he's dead with the spear. Jesus is in great pain, but he says, 'Father, forgive them, they don't know what they do.' Jesus forgives the soldiers and everyone who hurts him and lets him down. When Jesus dies, the Roman centurion soldier sees who Jesus is: 'Truly this man was the son of God'. **Important**: Put the eggs back in the box for the next group.)*

I wonder what it would be like to be a Roman soldier on Good Friday . . . They have a cruel job. They nail Jesus and the two criminals to wooden crosses and they stay on guard until they are all dead - they watch them suffer in great pain for six hours. They pass the time playing dice and gamble for Jesus' clothes. They're told to break the men's legs so that they will die quickly, but Jesus is already dead. A soldier thrusts a spear into Jesus' side to make sure he's dead, and out come blood and water, which show that he is already dead.

I wonder how Jesus feels about the soldiers . . . *(Jesus is in great pain, but before he dies, he forgives the soldiers and everyone who hurts him and lets him down.)*

Extra for Years 5 and 6 if needed

Do you think the soldiers are bad people? There are no wrong answers - just say what you think. *(The soldiers carry out their orders and do bad things without thinking.)*

(For all years.) Look at the picture of Good Friday. I wonder what you can see . . . I wonder how it makes you feel . . . Remember, there are no wrong answers - just say what you think.

Helper

Activity 1

Jesus forgives his friends who run away and the soldiers who hurt and kill him. It's not always easy to forgive people who let us down or hurt us. *(Give everyone a large nail to hold.)*

I wonder if anyone has let you down or hurt you . . . I wonder if there is anyone you need to forgive . . . Think about this, then put your nail at the foot of the cross/crucifix.

Helper

Activity 2

Colour the crosses and 'Father forgive' on the Easter egg card.

Helper

Activity (Years 5 and 6)

Imagine you are reporters for the *Jerusalem Herald* newspaper. Decide, as a group, on a headline for your newspaper for Good Friday. Write it down on a sticky note and stick it to the large piece of card with the heading 'Good Friday' on it. These will be shared at the end of the workshop and make a display to leave in church.

(For all years.) Is there anything you want to say or ask about the story? We may not have the answers, but we'll note down your questions. Some things about God are hard to understand.

Group 4: He is risen (10 minutes)

Helpers should read the story beforehand in Luke 24.1-12.

Materials required   Pens, labels, Easter egg cards to colour, sticky notes, large picture of Easter Day, six plastic eggs in an egg box filled with a piece of white cloth, small round stone, angel, chocolate egg and word 'Joy', leaving one egg empty; plus photocopies of scripts for play (see below) in plastic wallets or on card, tomb made from two chairs covered with a sheet or blanket and a large piece of card cut out for the stone.

Extra for Years 5 and 6 if needed

Large piece of card with the heading 'Easter Day' for sticky notes headlines.

Visual focus   Small table with large picture of Easter Day and egg box with the filled plastic eggs.

With the first group, make a name badge – just their first name, written clearly – and write their full name on a card.

Remember to keep ideas simple for Years 3 and 4, but expect more discussion with Years 5 and 6.

Helper   *(Let the children open the plastic eggs and say what they know about Easter Day, adding any bits they leave out or don't know, to explain the contents of the eggs. Include that, on Easter Day, Jesus' friends come to the tomb. The stone is rolled away, the tomb is empty, except for the burial cloth, and an angel says Jesus is alive. His friends are full of joy. Chocolate eggs remind us of new life and the empty tomb.* **Important:** *Put the eggs back in the box for the next group.)*

(Show the large Easter Day picture. NB: in Neil Thorogood's picture, Jesus does a cartwheel in the garden at sunrise!) I wonder what you can see . . . I wonder how it makes you feel . . . Remember, there are no wrong answers – just say what you think.

Let's look at the story now. *(Hand out the parts. See page 82 for the script.)*

Helper   No one knows how God raises Jesus from the dead, but Christians believe Jesus is alive and gives new life to people who follow him. Jesus' friends were sad and frightened when Jesus died, but happy and excited when they saw he was alive. Christians are happy and excited about Jesus today. Jesus gives us peace, hope and strength for living our lives.

Resurrection play: the empty tomb

(You will need an adult narrator, Mary, four bystanders, two soldiers and a priest. Have the children gather round an 'empty tomb' – made from two chairs covered with a sheet or blanket and a large piece of cut-out card to resemble a stone.)

Mary   Oh no! The tomb is empty, where has Jesus gone?

Bystander 1   Maybe Jesus wasn't dead after all.

Soldier 1   Look, I crucified Jesus. I do that for a living. He was dead all right. I know my job.

Bystander 2   Maybe his friends took him away.

Soldier 2   Oh no they didn't! I was on guard and Jesus' friends ran away. They're still hiding.

Bystander 3   Maybe the priests took Jesus' body away.

Priest   Why would we do that? We want everyone to know that Jesus is dead.

Everyone   Then where is Jesus?

Bystander 4   Maybe God raised Jesus to new life.

Mary   Jesus *is* alive – I've seen him in the garden.

Everyone   Hurray! Hurray! Jesus is risen! Jesus is alive!

Narrator   No one knows how God raises Jesus from the dead, but Christians believe that Jesus is alive and gives new life to people who follow him. Jesus' friends were sad and frightened when Jesus died, but happy and excited when they saw he was alive. Christians are happy and excited about Jesus today. Jesus gives us peace, hope and strength to live our lives.

RE Active Church (London: SPCK). Copyright © Jenny Gray 2012

Helper	**Activity**

Colour 'He is risen!' on the Easter egg card. *(Talk about Easter and what the children think happened at Easter.)*

Helper	**Activity (Years 5 and 6)**

Imagine you are reporters for the *Jerusalem Herald* newspaper. Decide, as a group, on a headline for your newspaper for Easter Day. Write it down on a sticky note and stick it to the large piece of card with the heading 'Easter Day' on it. These will be shared at the end of the workshop and make a display to leave in church.

(For all years.) Is there anything you want to say or ask about the story? We may not have the answers, but we'll note down your questions. Some things about God are hard to understand.

7
Jesus

In each school year, the RE curriculum will probably build on what children already know about Jesus. In Hertfordshire (at the time of writing), Year 3 focuses on stories about Jesus, his life and actions; Year 4 on the Bible; Year 5 looks at religious leaders, belief and certainty; Year 6 the importance of Jesus to Christians, expressing faith in art, drama and song. The topics covered in your local area will probably be similar.

This chapter sets out four one-hour workshops for Years 3–6 to explore the life and teaching of Jesus in church:

- Jesus' special prayer
- Four faces of Jesus
- Jesus changes lives
- Who is Jesus?

The teachers develop their own follow-up work for the workshops in school, according to their curriculum.

Workshop 1: Jesus' special prayer

Overview of workshop See the at-a-glance summary, page 118.

You will need
- Timer.
- CD player.
- CD of music (such as Taizé, Celtic, worship songs, spirituals) or CD of optional songs 'Kum By Yah', 'Father God in heaven',[1] or Caribbean versions of the Lord's Prayer.

For each class of 30: felt-tip pens, sticky labels, fizzy fish sweets, invitations, paper game to make (see template, Chapter 10), the Lord's Prayer on a card or as a PowerPoint slide.

For Group 1: toy fish, snake and scorpion, bread, stone, egg, soft modelling dough,[2] words 'Our Father in heaven, hallowed be your name' printed out, small table.

For Group 2: nine toy sheep, storybook[3] (for Years 3 and 4), large picture of shepherd (Turvey[4] or other), words 'Your will be done, on earth as in heaven' printed out, small table.

For Group 3: Loaf of bread, eight photocopies of play (see below) in plastic wallets or on card, Christian Aid or other charity posters, words 'Give us today our daily bread' printed out, small table.

For Group 4: story from the Brick New Testament[5] as PowerPoint slides or made into laminated cards, eight small trays of sand, words 'Forgive us, as we forgive' printed out.

Preparation	Play the CD as the children come in and leave. Set up four small-group areas, with the visual focus as indicated in the materials for each group (see below). Photocopy the notes for the helpers and gather together all the other materials required.

Craft

The children colour and fold the paper game photocopied from the template (see Chapter 10). It is a bit fiddly, but worth the effort!

In each small group, the children colour some of the pictures on the paper game. At the end, they need to fold the outside triangles (along line 1) back so that the pictures are on one side and the words are on the other. Fold the triangles inwards to cover the words on the small square along line 2. Finally, fold the paper in half and half again to make a tiny square, which the children open out and insert their forefingers and thumbs under the pictures.

Each child is also given a separate invitation to church activities with the words of the Lord's Prayer. There is space to include the address of the church website (and joint town churches' website), if available, to help parents and children follow up the experience in church.

Leader

Introduction to each class (5 minutes)

(Welcome the children at the church door and lead them to the pews or seats at the front of the church. Invite them to put their coats and so on under the pews or seats to be collected at the end of the session.)

Welcome to our 'Jesus' special prayer' workshop.

Your teacher will put you into four small groups to go round each activity. The buzzer will tell us when to change.

We'll give you a sticky label to write your name on, so we know who you are – just your first name as clearly as you can. The team members have their labels on already – let me introduce them to you now . . .

Prayer is part of all religions. I wonder what you know about prayer, what it is, how people do it, where and when . . . *(Acknowledge any ideas.)*

Jesus prayed every day. His friends, the disciples, asked Jesus to teach them to pray too. Jesus gives them a special prayer – one that Christians still pray today. I wonder if you know what it's called . . . *(The Lord's Prayer or Our Father.)*

We're going to find out about this special prayer in our four small group activities and you'll be given a special Lord's Prayer game to make, adding to it as you go round the groups *(show)*. We hope you'll show people at home your special game and tell them what you did in church today.

Leader

Conclusion to each session (15 minutes)

I wonder how much of the Lord's Prayer you remember from today. Your game will help you . . .

> Our Father in heaven, hallowed be your name,
> your kingdom come, your will be done, on earth as in heaven.
> Give us today our daily bread,
> forgive us our sins as we forgive those who sin against us.

The Lord's Prayer doesn't end here, though – does anyone know how it ends . . . ?

> Lead us not into temptation but deliver us from evil.
> For the kingdom, the power and the glory are yours, now and for ever. Amen.

Jesus tells us that we can ask God to help us do the right thing when we're tempted to do wrong.

The prayer ends with a reminder that the world and everything in it comes from God – 'the kingdom, the power and the glory are yours, now and for ever. Amen'.

We can put the whole Lord's Prayer together with actions. Stand up and join in with me.

Our Father in heaven	*(both hands stretched up high)*,
hallowed be your name	*(both hands down in front of waist, palms up)*,
your kingdom come	*(one arm out to side, bent at elbow, fist clenched)*,
your will be done	*(other arm out to side, bent at elbow, fist clenched)*,
on earth as in heaven	*(hands reaching up to make a circle)*.
Give us today our daily bread	*(hands together in front of waist, palms up)*,
forgive us our sins	*(hands together in front, pointing up in prayer)*
as we forgive those who sin against us	*(hands stay together in front in prayer)*.
Lead us not into temptation	*(hands in front, palms down at waist height, move out to side)*
but deliver us from evil	*(hands move back to centre, overlapping, several times)*.
For the kingdom	*(one arm out to side, bent at elbow, fist clenched)*,
the power	*(other arm out to side, bent at elbow, fist clenched)*
and the glory are yours	*(both hands pointing up and waving on the spot)*,
now and for ever. Amen.	*(continue above action)*.

(Repeat if the children want to and there is time.)

We'll end with a version of the Lord's Prayer written like a text message *(show card or PowerPoint slide)*. You can join in with me.

Dad@hvn, ur spshl.
We want wot u want
& urth 2b like hvn
Giv us food
& 4giv us, lyk we 4giv uvaz.
Don't test us! Save us!
Bcos we kno ur boss,
Ur tuf, ur cool, 4 eva! OK

Texting the Lord's Prayer reminds us that prayer is like a telephone, for us to talk to God. We can pray to God anytime, anywhere, every day. We can talk out loud or say no words at all, but God will always hear our call, always hear our prayer. We don't need a special contract, we don't need to be in church – everyone can pray to God, everywhere. We can ask for his help, say 'sorry' and 'thank you' every day. We can also pray the special prayer we learned today to keep in touch with God.

*(**Optional song**: 'Kum By Yah' or Caribbean versions of the Lord's Prayer.)*

(Ask helpers for any interesting questions or comments.)

Thank you for working so well today. We'll leave the text version of the Lord's Prayer and a Lord's Prayer game in church so the congregation can see on Sunday what you have been doing with us. Enjoy your little fish when your teacher says you can eat it. Don't forget your invitation to *(mention any summer activities or groups as appropriate)*. Happy summer to you all.

Group 1: Our Father in heaven, hallowed be your name (10 minutes)

Helpers should read the story beforehand in Matthew 7.7-11.

Materials required Pens, labels, paper game to make, toy fish, snake and scorpion, bread, stone, egg, soft modelling dough, words 'Our Father in heaven, hallowed be your name' printed out, small table.

Visual focus Small table with toy fish, snake and scorpion, bread, stone, egg, soft modelling dough, words 'Our Father in heaven, hallowed be your name' printed out.

With the first group, make a name badge – just their first name, written clearly – and write their full name on a game.

Remember to keep ideas simple for Years 3 and 4, but expect more discussion with Years 5 and 6.

Helper I wonder what a good parent is like . . . (*Loving, kind, generous, patient, always there, plays, helps, listens, encourages, supports, teaches, gives you rules, keeps us safe, wants the best for us.*)

I wonder if any parent is perfect . . . (*However much they love us, however hard they try, our mums and dads aren't perfect – sometimes they're too busy, not around or don't understand.*)

Jesus shows us God is the perfect parent – better than the best father or mother we can imagine. We can't see God, but Jesus shows us what God is like. God loves each one of us. God wants the best for us. God's always there for us. If we ask him, God will always help us.

God isn't scary or far away, as some people think. God is our perfect Father in heaven.

(*With props in each hand.*) Jesus says:

- 'If your child asks for a *fish* will you give him a *snake*?' (*No.*)
- 'If your child asks for *bread* will you give him *a stone*?' (*No.*)
- 'If your child asks for an *egg* will you give him a *scorpion*?' (*No.*)

If human parents care for their children and want the best for them, we can trust God, our Heavenly Father, to look after us and want the best for us. So Jesus begins his special prayer: 'Our Father in heaven'.

Helper ### Activity 1

(*Make a fish from the soft modelling dough and turn it into a snake and so on. Give the children pieces of the dough to shape and, meanwhile, talk about the next part of the Lord's Prayer, pointing it out in the display.*) 'Hallowed be your name' – I wonder what 'hallowed' means . . . (*Respect and honour God, keep his name special.*)

I wonder who you respect and honour . . . (*Maybe parents, teachers, the Queen, the Pope, doctors.*)

I wonder why Jesus tells us to respect and honour God . . . (*God made the world and everything in it.*)

I wonder how we hallow God's name . . . (*Not swear, sing hymns and say prayers to worship him, try to do what he asks, be like him, like Jesus.*)

Helper ### Activity 2

Find 'Our Father in heaven' on the game and colour the snake and fish. (*With the last group, fold the outside triangles (along line 1) back so that the pictures are on one side and the words are on the other. Fold the triangles inwards to cover the words on the small square along line 2. Finally, fold the paper in half and half again to make a tiny square, which the children open out and insert their forefingers and thumbs under the pictures.)*

Is there anything you want to say or ask? We may not have the answers, but we'll note down your questions. Some things about God are hard to understand.

Group 2: Your will be done, on earth as it is in heaven (10 minutes)

Helpers should read the story beforehand in Luke 15.1-7.

Materials required   Pens, labels, paper game to make, nine toy sheep, storybook (for Years 3 and 4), large picture of shepherd (Turvey or other), words 'Your will be done, on earth as it is in heaven' printed out, small table.

Visual focus   Small table with large picture of shepherd and words 'Your will be done, on earth as it is in heaven' printed out.

With the first group, make a name badge - just their first name, written clearly - and write their full name on a game.

Remember to keep ideas simple for Years 3 and 4, but expect more discussion with Years 5 and 6.

Helper   *(Hide eight of the sheep, keeping one in your pocket.)* I've lost all my sheep. I need you to find my missing sheep - just one sheep per person. You can sit down when you've found a sheep. *(Count up the sheep as the children find them.)* O dear - one sheep is still missing! I'll see if I can find it. . . . *(Have a quick look round and 'find' it.)*

'Hurray! I love all my sheep. I don't want to lose a single one.' Jesus tells a story about a lost sheep. *(Tell it using a storybook, from memory or from the Bible.)*

(Show large picture of shepherd.) We do/don't see shepherds with sheep where we live *(adapt according to your area)*. I wonder what shepherds do . . . *(Include that they care for all their sheep, feed them, keep them safe from wild animals and thieves, know them by name.)*

A shepherd is like your teacher. Your teacher knows you all by name and keeps a register. When the fire alarm goes off, you go outside and your teacher checks everyone is safe. If just one child was missing, the firefighters would go into the school to rescue the child because every child matters. Everyone would be happy when that child was saved.

God is like your teacher or firefighters. Like a good shepherd, God cares for every human being. God doesn't want anyone to be lost or left out. Jesus cares for everyone, especially people no one else thinks are important. I wonder who might seem not to matter . . . *(Children, women, poor people, sick people, lepers, foreigners, especially Samaritans and Romans at the time of the Bible, tax collectors, prostitutes, drug dealers or addicts today.)* Jesus cares for all these people, he helps them, heals them, shares meals with them and welcomes them as his friends.

Have you ever noticed someone being left out or maybe you've felt left out yourself . . . I wonder how you'd feel if you were left out . . .

I wonder what we can do to make sure people are not left out . . .

I'm sorry you can't keep the sheep - I need you to hide them for the next group to find.

Helper   **Activity**

Find 'Your will be done' on the game and colour the sheep. (*With the last group, fold the outside triangles (along line 1) back so that the pictures are on one side and the words are on the other. Fold the triangles inwards to cover the words on the small square along line 2. Finally, fold the paper in half and half again to make a tiny square, which the children open out and insert their forefingers and thumbs under the pictures.*)

Is there anything you want to say or ask? We may not have the answers, but we'll note down your questions. Some things about God are hard to understand.

Group 3: Give us today our daily bread (10 minutes)

Helpers should read the story beforehand in Luke 12.13-21.

Materials required   Pens, labels, paper game to make, loaf of bread, eight photocopies of play (see below) in plastic wallets or on card, Christian Aid or other charity posters, words 'Give us today our daily bread' printed out, small table.

Visual focus   Small table with Christian Aid or other poster and words 'Give us today our daily bread' printed out.

With the first group, make a name badge - just their first name, written clearly - and write their full name on a game.

Remember to keep ideas simple for Years 3 and 4, but expect more discussion with Years 5 and 6.

Helper   Take a look at the words in our display - 'Give us today our daily bread'. (*Give one child the loaf.*) There's your daily bread - is that OK? Is everyone happy? Is this fair? Do you think this is how God wants the world to be? (*Discuss and look at some charity posters.*)

Jesus tells a story about a rich farmer who keeps everything for himself - we're going to act it out. (*Hand out the parts. See page 90 for the script.*)

I wonder what you think about the story . . . I wonder what makes you happy . . .

Jesus says the way to be happy is to think about other people, not just yourself, and try to make the world fair and good for everyone. God doesn't want anyone to be hungry or homeless or sad or lonely; he wants everyone to be able to go to school, to the doctor, to have time to play and enjoy our beautiful world. I wonder how this can happen . . . (*We need to care and share, help people in need, support charities like Christian Aid.*)

Helper   **Activity**

Find 'Give us today our daily bread' on the game and colour the bread. (*With the last group, fold the outside triangles (along line 1) back so that the pictures are on one side and the words are on the other. Fold the triangles inwards to cover the words on the small square along line 2. Finally, fold the paper in half and half again to make a tiny square, which the children open out and insert their forefingers and thumbs under the pictures.*)

Is there anything you want to say or ask? We may not have the answers, but we'll note down your questions. Some things about God are hard to understand.

Building bigger barns

(You will need a narrator, farmer (may be an adult), God, a small barn (1 child, hands joined above his or her head) a bigger barn (two children with their hands joined above their heads) and an enormous barn (everyone who's left, hands joined together).)

Narrator	Once there was a farmer who grew good crops, but he only had a little barn to put them in.
Small barn	I've got room for all the food you need.
Farmer	This little barn isn't big enough for all my crops. I'll flatten it *(child drops to the ground)* and build a big barn.
Big barn	I've got room to store food for the whole town.
Farmer	This big barn isn't big enough for all my crops. I'll flatten it *(children drop to ground)* and build an enormous barn.
Enormous barn	I've got room to store food for the whole country.
Farmer	I'm so lucky, I'm so rich, I can take life easy and enjoy myself.
God	You silly man. You're going to die tonight. Then who will enjoy the crops you've stored in your barns?

Group 4: Forgive us, as we forgive (10 minutes)

Helpers should read the story beforehand in Matthew 18.21–35.

Materials required   Pens, labels, paper game to make, story from the Brick New Testament as PowerPoint slides or made into laminated cards, eight small trays of sand, words 'Forgive us, as we forgive' printed out.

Visual focus   Tray of sand and words 'Forgive us, as we forgive' printed out.

With the first group, make a name badge – just their first name, written clearly – and write their full name on a game.

Remember to keep ideas simple for Years 3 and 4, but expect more discussion with Years 5 and 6.

Helper   We'll begin with a forgiveness quiz. How easy is it to forgive people? We will use a scale of one to three, where one is easy and three is difficult. Let's see what you think the rating for these situations should be.

- A friend borrows your rubber and doesn't give it back.
- Your friend doesn't invite you to his or her party.
- You catch your friend disrespecting you.

Our forgiveness quiz shows us that some things are easy and some things are hard to forgive. I wonder if you've ever found it difficult to forgive someone . . .

Jesus tells a story about forgiveness. *(Tell the Brick New Testament story.)*

I wonder what you think about the story . . .

Extra for Years 5 and 6 if needed

(If there is time.) I wonder how it feels if we can't forgive someone . . .

I wonder how it feels if someone won't forgive us . . .

Helper   ### Activity 1

When we say sorry to God, he always forgives us and forgets what we've done wrong – like wiping out writing in sand *(show using sand in tray)*. We'll be quiet for a moment and think about anything we are sorry for doing or saying or not doing . . . If you want to, you can write or draw in the sand, then wipe it away as a sign that God forgives you when you're sorry and forgets what you've done wrong.

Helper   ### Activity 2

Find 'Forgive us and help us forgive others' on the game and colour the money. *(With the last group, fold the outside triangles (along line 1) back so that the pictures are on one side and the words are on the other. Fold the triangles inwards to cover the words on the small square along line 2. Finally, fold the paper in half and half again to make a tiny square, which the children open out and insert their forefingers and thumbs under the pictures.)*

Is there anything you want to say or ask? We may not have the answers, but we'll note down your questions. Some things about God are hard to understand.

Workshop 2: Four faces of Jesus

Overview of workshop   See the at-a-glance summary, page 118.

You will need
- Timer.
- CD player.
- CD of music (such as Taizé, Celtic, worship songs, spirituals) or CD of optional song 'Our God is a great big God'.[6]

For each class of 30: felt-tip pens, sticky labels, A4 card crosses (see template, Chapter 10), little pig sweets.

For Group 1: pictures of the faces of famous people[7] (choose depending on who is popular, in the news and so on) or buy masks of them, egg timer, wool, glue sticks, large picture of Jesus with children (Turvey[8] or other).

For Group 2: eight photocopies of the play (see below) in plastic wallets or on card, gel pens or glitter glue, oval or round sticky notes (that is, like the shapes of pills), medicine bottle-shape, cut out of cardboard, as a prayer board.

For Group 3: wedding hats for girls and simple top hats for boys, red juice or squash, 2 jugs of water, 2 opaque jugs, 1 wine bottle, 16 plastic wine glasses (that is, 2 sets of jugs and glasses so that they can be washed and refilled between groups), 60 googly eyes, large picture of Jesus laughing,[9] small table.

For Group 4: lost rabbit, dog or cat poster, beard, bag of money, party hats, plastic glasses, pig masks, toy pigs or pictures of pigs, microphone, 60 small heart stickers, picture of Rembrandt's *Return of the Prodigal Son* painting.[10]

Preparation   Play the CD of songs as the children come in and leave. Set up four small-group areas with the visual focus as indicated in the materials for each group (see below). Photocopy the notes for the helpers and gather together all the other materials required, adding invitations to the back of the crosses and cutting them out.

Craft   The children add to the four faces on the A4 cross template (see Chapter 10) with words and text. There is space to add invitations on the back of the crosses and include the address of the church website (and joint town churches' website), if available, on the back to help parents and children follow up the experience in church.

Leader

Introduction to each class (5 minutes)

(Welcome the children at the church door and lead them to the pews or seats at the front of the church. Invite them to put their coats and so on under the pews or seats to be collected at the end of the session.)

Welcome to our 'Four faces of Jesus' workshop. Jesus is born at Christmas, dies and rises to new life at Easter, but what happens in between? What does Jesus do in his life? What is Jesus like . . . ? *(Let the children answer without commenting or adding other ideas. They may include that Jesus tells stories, teaches, does miracles, heals, makes friends with people who are left out, forgives, helps, shows what God is like, is God with us.)*

We'll see what else you find out as you go round the groups today. Your teacher will put you into four small groups to go round each activity. The buzzer will tell us when to change.

We'll give you a sticky label to write your name on, so we know who you are – just your first name as clearly as you can. The team members have their labels on already – let me introduce them to you now . . . You will also be given a special cross with four faces for you to add to as you go round each group *(show)*. We hope you'll show people at home your special cross and tell them what you did in church today.

Leader

Conclusion to each session (15 minutes)

Let's see what you found out today about Jesus – what he does and what he's like . . . (*Include that Jesus makes people well, tells stories, shows us how to live, does miracles, heals, welcomes children, helps people enjoy life, Jesus shares our feelings, he gets angry and sad, laughs and loves like we do.*)

Jesus is like us and he's like God. Jesus shows us what God, our heavenly Father, is like and how God feels too. Jesus says 'Whoever has seen me has seen the Father.' You'll find these words on your cross.

So now we're going to close our eyes to do some thinking and feeling – closing our eyes helps us concentrate.

First, think of something that makes you happy – something you enjoy, makes you smile, maybe something beautiful or funny, or having a good time with your friends . . . Jesus likes being with his friends too – he enjoys parties and wants people to have fun. So does God. God wants us to be happy and enjoy the beautiful world he's made.

Now think of something that makes you sad, makes you cry . . . Jesus feels sad when people are sick and unhappy, when they hurt each other, when people are left out. That's how God feels too. God wants us to do what we can to help.

Now think of something that makes you angry, maybe when something's wrong or unfair . . . Jesus feels angry when people do wrong, when they're unkind or unfair. That's how God feels too. God wants us to do what we can to put things right.

Last, think of someone you love . . . That's how Jesus feels about you and me and every person in the world. That's how God feels too.

(**Optional song**: 'Our God is a great big God'.)

(*Ask helpers for any interesting questions or comments.*)

Thank you for working so well today. We're going to leave the medicine bottle prayer board in church so the congregation can see on Sunday what you have been doing with us. Enjoy your little pig sweet when your teacher says you can eat it. Don't forget your invitation to (*mention any special summer activities or groups, as appropriate*). Happy summer to you all.

Group 1: Angry Jesus – who is the greatest? (10 minutes)

Helpers should read the story beforehand in Luke 9.46–48 and Matthew 18.1–5 or Mark 10.33–37. We chose this story rather than Jesus being angry in the Temple or with sickness and death, because it's about a child and shows how much children matter to God.

Materials required   Pens, labels, card crosses to colour, pictures of the faces of famous people or buy masks of such people, egg timer, wool, glue sticks, large picture of Jesus with children (Turvey or other).

Visual focus   Large picture of Jesus with children.

With the first group, make a name badge – just their first name, written clearly – and write their full name on a cross.

Remember to keep ideas simple for Years 3 and 4, but expect more discussion with Years 5 and 6.

Helper   (*Give children a famous person or mask each – except for one child, who can be him- or herself. If there is another extra child, he or she can be in charge of the egg timer and* *share in the discussion.)* I wonder which of these people is the most important . . . You can talk about it together and put yourselves in a line, with the most important person at the front, the least important at the back. You have a three-minute time limit in which to do this. There are no wrong answers – just do what you think.

(After three minutes.) You need to put the spare child(ren) in your line. I wonder where this person/these people should be . . . *(The children may say last, right at the back.)*

Jesus says children are very important. *(Move the child(ren) to the front of the line.)* I wonder how you feel about this . . . *(Maybe surprised, pleased, agree or disagree.)*

(Sit down, show the large picture of Jesus with the children and tell the story of Jesus and the little child.) Jesus' friends, the disciples, argue about who is the most important, which of them will sit next to Jesus. Jesus is angry and disappointed with them. He shows them a little child. He says that little children are important to God, not the people who think they are important. I wonder how the disciples feel about this . . . *(Surprised, confused, ashamed, angry.)*

Jesus says that we should all be like a little child. I wonder what he means . . . I wonder what qualities children have that grown-ups often lose . . . *(They accept people, are not worried about the kind of house, car, clothes, jobs people have, trust people, adventurous, like to explore, ask questions and try new things, enjoy the present and don't worry about tomorrow, are honest, don't pretend, get excited and wonder.)*

Jesus goes on to tell the disciples that the greatest people are those who serve other people. I wonder who you know who serves other people – maybe they have low-paid jobs or don't get paid at all . . . *(Mums, carers in families or care homes, helpers in schools, cleaners.)* Jesus says that *all* these people are really important.

Helper   **Activity**

Jesus is angry when we put other people down, when we think that we're the most important.

Make an angry face. Now stick a wool frown on the angry face on your cross. Is there anything you want to say or ask about the story? We may not have the answers, but we'll note down your questions. Some things about God are hard to understand.

Group 2: Crying Jesus – healing Jairus' daughter (10 minutes)

Helpers should read the story beforehand in Matthew 9.18-19 and 23-26, plus Mark 5.22-24 and 35-43, also Luke 8.41-42 and 49-56. We chose this story rather than the raising of Lazarus because it is about a child and shows how much children matter to God.

Materials required   Pens, labels, card crosses to colour, eight photocopies of the play (see below) in plastic wallets or on card, gel pens or glitter glue, oval or round sticky notes (that is, like the shapes of pills), medicine bottle-shaped cardboard prayer board.

Visual focus   Medicine bottle-shaped prayer board.

With the first group, make a name badge – just their first name, written clearly – and write their full name on a cross.

Remember to keep ideas simple for Years 3 and 4, but expect more discussion with Years 5 and 6.

Healing Jairus' daughter

(You will need a narrator, a mother, Jairus, Jesus, Jairus' friends and a crowd.)

Narrator	Jairus is important. He's the leader of a synagogue, which is a Jewish church. He has a little girl who's twelve years old and very ill.
Mother	The doctors can't make our little girl well. I think she's going to die.
Jairus	I'll get Jesus. Jesus makes people well.
Mother	Lots of people want Jesus' help. Will he bother with our little girl?
Jairus	Jesus cares for everyone, especially children.
Narrator	Jairus finds Jesus and begs him to come with him. Jesus agrees.
Jairus' friends	Stop Jairus. Your little girl is dead. Don't bother Jesus now.
Jesus	Don't be afraid, Jairus. Trust me.
Crowd	You're too late. His little girl is dead.
Narrator	Jesus goes to Jairus' house. Everyone is crying.
Jesus	Stop crying. This little girl's not dead, she's asleep.
Mother	She is dead. Come and see.
Narrator	Jesus goes to the little girl's room and takes her hand.
Jesus	Little girl, get up.
Narrator	Immediately, the little girl gets up and walks.
Jesus	Now give her something to eat.
Everyone	Jesus has made Jairus' little girl well. It's a miracle.

RE Active Church (London: SPCK). Copyright © Jenny Gray 2012

Helper	Imagine you're not feeling very well. I wonder what might help you feel better . . . *(Parents, doctors, nurses, hospitals, medicines, good food, drinks, visitors, cards, presents.)*
	Christians believe that prayer helps people feel better too. We pray for people who are sick because we believe God cares about them. The Bible has lots of stories about Jesus making sick people well. The play we are about to do is the story of Jesus healing a twelve-year-old girl – Jairus' daughter. *(Hand out the parts. See page 95 for the script.)*
	Jairus brings Jesus to his little girl. We can't go and get Jesus now, but we can ask Jesus to help people who are sick or in trouble in our prayers. I wonder if you ask God to help people, if you pray for people . . .
	Prayer is complicated. It's not like a slot machine and we can't tell God what to do. Only God knows what's best for each person. Sometimes the people we pray for get better, sometimes they don't, but God cares about everyone. Whatever our problems, Christians believe that God gives us peace and hope, God supports and helps us, but God doesn't want us to leave it all to him. He wants us to help people too. I wonder how we can help people who are sick . . . *(Medicines, doctors, visits, phone calls, show we care.)*
Helper	**Activity 1**
	If you like, you can write the name of someone you know who is sick or in trouble on a sticky note that's in the shape of a pill, and add it to our medicine bottle prayer board to leave in church. Is there anyone who needs God's help? Remember, Jesus wants us to help them too.
Helper	**Activity 2**
	Make a sad face. Jesus is sad when we are sad. Add tears to the sad face on your cross using the gel pens or glitter glue. Is there anything you want to say or ask about the story? We may not have the answers, but we'll note down your questions. Some things about God are hard to understand.

Group 3: Laughing Jesus – the wedding at Cana (10 minutes)

	Helpers should read the story beforehand in John 2.1-11.
Materials required	Pens, labels, card crosses to colour, wedding hats for girls and simple top hats for boys, red juice or squash, 2 jugs of water, 2 opaque jugs, 1 wine bottle, 16 plastic wine glasses (that is, 2 sets of jugs and glasses so that they can be washed and refilled between groups), 60 googly eyes, large picture of Jesus laughing, small table.
Visual focus	Small table with large picture of Jesus laughing, wine bottle, glass, wedding hat.
	With the first group, make a name badge – just their first name, written clearly – and write their full name on a cross.
	Remember to keep ideas simple for Years 3 and 4, but expect more discussion with Years 5 and 6.
Helper	*(Invite the children to sit in a circle.)* Close your eyes for a moment and picture Jesus . . . I wonder how you see his face – is he smiling, happy, kind, solemn, sad, fierce . . . ?
	Some people think Jesus is serious all the time, but Jesus has friends, he laughs and smiles and has a good time, he enjoys meals with his friends and goes to parties like us and he tells funny stories. *(Show picture of Jesus laughing.)* I wonder what you feel about the picture . . .

We're going to a party with Jesus, his friends and his mother Mary – a wedding at Cana in Galilee. You need special clothes for a wedding *(give out hats)* and the grown-ups like to have wine to drink *(give out a plastic wine glass to each child)*. Everyone is having a lovely time at this wedding. Then something terrible happens – the wine runs out. Jesus' mother asks Jesus to help. Jesus tells the waiters to fill six great big stone jars with water and pour some into a jug for the head waiter to taste *(pour some water from a clear jug into an opaque jug with red juice or squash at the bottom, then pour a little into a glass, so the children see clear water going into the jug and 'wine' poured out – a miracle)*.

The head waiter tries it *(taste it)*. He doesn't know where it's come from, but it's delicious, the best wine he's ever tasted. He tells the waiters to serve it to the guests. *(Pour some for everyone into the plastic wine glasses.)* It's a miracle – a sign that Jesus is God with us. I wonder what this miracle of turning water into wine at a wedding tells us about Jesus and about God . . .

Jesus is special. His mother, Mary, knows Jesus is special from what the angels, shepherds and wise men said at his birth, which is why she asked him to help. Now his friends know it too.

Jesus shows that God cares about everyday things, like wine running out at a wedding. Jesus shows that God is generous – there's much more wine than they need. Jesus shows us that God wants us to enjoy life. God's not a spoilsport. God's made the world with wonderful things for us to enjoy – but we have to look after the world too.

Following Jesus isn't boring. Life with Jesus is like drinking the best drink you can imagine, the best smoothie or fizzy drink – life without Jesus is like drinking plain water.

Weddings are special to people and this is where Jesus performed his first miracle or sign.

Extra work for Years 5 and 6 if needed
Changing water into wine is a miracle. Different people have different ideas about miracles – whether they actually happen or can be explained away.[11] I wonder what you think . . .

Helper

Activity

Jesus laughs like us. Smile. Now, stick googly eyes on to the smiling face on your cross. Is there anything you want to say or ask about the story? We may not have the answers, but we'll note down your questions. Some things about God are hard to understand.

Group 4: Loving Jesus – the prodigal son (10 minutes)

Helpers should read the story beforehand in Luke 15.11–24.

Materials required   Pens, labels, card crosses to colour, lost rabbit, dog or cat poster, beard, bag of money, party hats, plastic glasses, pig masks, toy pigs or pictures of pigs, microphone, 60 small heart stickers, picture of Rembrandt's *Return of the Prodigal Son* painting.

Visual focus   Picture of Rembrandt's *Return of the Prodigal Son* painting.

With the first group, make a name badge – just their first name, written clearly – and write their full name on a cross.

Remember to keep ideas simple for Years 3 and 4, but expect more discussion with Years 5 and 6.

Helper

I wonder if you've seen a poster like this near your house or school . . . *(show lost rabbit, dog or cat poster).*

I wonder why people make posters like this . . . *(We love pets, they're part of the family, so if they're lost, we want to find them, even offer a reward for their return.)*

Jesus tells stories about losing and finding things that are important. Today, we'll find out about a lost son. You can be part of the story.

I need one of you to be a dad and another to be his son . . . *(give out the beard and bag of money to the dad)* two or three people to be friends . . . *(give them party hats and plastic glasses and send them to one corner of the room)* two or three people to be pigs . . . *(give them pig masks, toy pigs or pictures of pigs and send them to the other side of the room).*

As I tell the story, you need to listen for your character and be ready to move around the room. I'm going to tell the story and be a news reporter, with my microphone *(show)*, ready to interview you about what's happening.

One day, a boy asks his dad to give him the money he'd receive when his dad dies. The dad hands the money over without a word *(dad hands bag of money to son)*. I wonder how the father feels . . . *(use the microphone to interview the father and anyone else who wants to say what they think)*. Remember, there are no wrong answers . . . *(Maybe hurt, angry, sad, disappointed, surprised.)*

The son leaves home with the money and waves goodbye *(son waves)*. He goes to a far country and makes new friends *(son goes to corner of the room)*. He spends his money on parties and drinks *(friends drink)*. He has a good time, but then his money runs out *(son hands money to friends)*. His friends leave him *(they wave goodbye and go back to his father)*.

The son has nowhere to live, nothing to eat. He's in a mess. I wonder how the son feels now . . . *(use microphone to interview the son and anyone else who wants to say what they think . . . worried, ashamed, depressed)*.

The son gets a job no one wants, looking after pigs *(son goes to the corner with the pigs, who make pig noises)*. He's so hungry, he could eat the pigs' food. Yuck! He thinks about home. His dad's servants have good food to eat. He could say sorry and ask to be his dad's servant. His dad is sure to be angry and won't want him as a son, but maybe he should go home . . . *(use microphone to interview the son, then anyone else who wants to say what they think)*.

The son decides to go home *(son goes across to dad)*.

When the dad sees his son, he runs to meet him, hugs him and organizes a big party to celebrate his return *(friends all drink)*.

I wonder why the dad is so good to his son . . . *(use microphone to interview the dad and anyone else who wants to say what they think . . . his dad loves his son, he's so happy he's home, he missed him, worried about him)*.

I wonder how the son feels about this lovely welcome . . . *(use microphone to interview the son and anyone else who wants to say what they think . . . surprised, happy, relieved)*.

(Sit down in a circle.) I wonder who the dad in Jesus' story is meant to be . . . *(God)*.

I wonder who the son in the story is meant to be . . . *(people who ignore God, think money and power all that matter, get in a mess, drink or drug addicts, criminals.)*

I wonder what the story tells us about God . . . (*God's a loving father, he cares about us, forgives us when we do wrong, welcomes us back. God loves us, but lets us choose how we live and what we believe.*)

The son thinks money and parties will make him happy. I wonder what makes you happy . . .

Helper | **Activity**

Stick the heart stickers to the loving face on the cross as cheeks. Is there anything you want to say or ask about the story? We may not have the answers, but we'll note down your questions. Some things about God are hard to understand.

Extra for Years 5 and 6 if needed

Look at Rembrandt's painting. I wonder what you can see in the picture . . . I wonder how you feel about the picture . . .

Workshop 3: Jesus changes lives

Overview of workshop   See the at-a-glance summary, page 118.

You will need
- Timer.
- CD player.
- CD of music (such as Taizé, Celtic, worship songs, spirituals) or CD of optional song 'Hosanna',[12] one verse of 'Put your hand in the hand of the man who stilled the waters'[13] or 'Jesus is a friend of mine',[14] plus the *Neighbours* theme tune, if using.

For each class of 30: felt-tip pens, sticky labels, colour-by-letters worksheets (see template, Chapter 10), handkerchief, two clear mixing bowls of water, rubber gloves, iodine drops (available from chemists), photographic fluid or a few drops of the dechlorinator sodium thiosulphate used in swimming pools (available from companies that supply chemicals to swimming pools), large pictures of the good Samaritan, the feeding of the five thousand, Zacchaeus, 'gentle Jesus' and, the 'Meek. Mild. As if.' Che Guevara Jesus,[15] Turvey[16] or other.

For Group 1: hobby horse (optional), bandages, money bag, eight photocopies of the play in plastic wallets or on card, five baseball hats – labelled 'Priest', 'Teacher', 'Samaritan', 'Innkeeper' and 'Jesus' (optional).

For Group 2: people outline cards (laminated), washable pens, wipes, feel good and feel bad cards (A5 cards, laminated, to include a picture of flowers, fruit, medicine, praying hands, a sport, cake, wine, pet, sad face with words 'I'm all alone' and a TV), bandages, trellis cross[17] (also used in 'Easter friends' workshop).

For Group 3: Christian Aid or other charity posters, picture of or toy chicken, box of eggs.

For Group 4: jar marked 'Romans', jar marked 'Me', effervescent vitamin tablets and four big test tubes with some water in them, small table, 30 wrapped sweets.

Preparation   Play the CD of songs as the children come in and leave. Set up four small-group areas, with the visual focus as indicated in the materials for each group (see below). Photocopy the notes for the helpers and gather together all the other materials required.

Craft
The children fill in the colour-by-letters worksheets. There is a simpler template for Years 3 and 4 and a more complex one for Years 5 and 6 (see Chapter 10). On the back, there is a Bible text and an invitation to church activities. There is space to include the address of the church website (and joint town churches' website), if available, to help parents and children follow up the experience in church.

Leader

Introduction to each class (5 minutes)

(Welcome the children at the church door and lead them to the pews or seats at the front of the church. Invite them to put their coats and so on under the pews or seats to be collected at the end of the session.)

Welcome to our 'Jesus changes lives' workshop. Jesus made a difference to people long ago and still does to people today.

Your teacher will put you into four small groups to go round each activity. The buzzer will tell us when to change.

We'll give you a sticky label to write your name on, so we know who you are – just your first name as clearly as you can. The team members have their labels on already – let me introduce them to you now . . . You will also be given a special colour-by-letters sheet for you to fill in as you go round the groups *(show)*. We hope you'll show people at home your sheet and tell them what you did in church today.

Leader

Conclusion to each session (15 minutes)

Let's see what you found out today about Jesus – what he does and what he's like . . . *(He changes people from baddy to goody, sick to well, small to big, enemy to friend.)*

There aren't any pictures of Jesus when he was alive, but lots of people paint pictures of Jesus. Some people imagine Jesus like this . . . *(show the 'gentle Jesus' picture and the 'Meek. Mild. As if.' Jesus based on Che Guevara)*. I wonder what you think about these two pictures. I wonder what they say about Jesus . . .

Jesus is revolutionary – he upsets respectable people and changes people's lives. He makes friends with outsiders, like Samaritans and tax collectors. He touches untouchables, like lepers. He feeds the hungry. He forgives the things we do wrong. He makes sick people well.

He brings out the best in people. He helps people get the most out of life. Jesus says, 'I have come so you may have life, in all its fullness.' You'll find those words on the back of your sheet.

Jesus shows that God loves everyone, especially people who are left out. Jesus wants us to be like him. It's not easy, but Christians try to be like Jesus. Christians have led campaigns to abolish slavery, reform prisons and set up schools for children. Christians set up charities like Shelter for homeless people and The Samaritans for people who've given up.

Christians believe that Jesus changes lives today. *(Demonstrate with the handkerchief and two clear mixing bowls of water, adding a few drops of iodine to one and a few drops of photographic fluid or sodium thiosulphate to the other. With the rubber gloves on, put the handkerchief into the water with the iodine drops added.)* This cloth is now dirty – like us when we're selfish and greedy, when we take more than we need and don't help people.

(Put the dirty handkerchief in the water to which the photographic fluid or sodium thiosulphate has been added.) Now the cloth is clean – like us when Jesus forgives the things we do wrong and helps us to be kind and loving like him. Christians believe that Jesus brings out the best in us and helps us get the best out of life. Each of us can be like Jesus and help to make the world a better place.

*(**Optional song**: 'Hosanna', one verse of 'Put your hand in the hand of the man who stilled the waters' or 'Jesus is a friend of mine'.)*

(Ask helpers for any interesting questions or comments.)

Thank you for working so well today. We'll leave the trellis cross with your prayer bandages in church so the congregation can see on Sunday what you have been doing with us. Enjoy your sweet when your teacher says you can eat it. Don't forget your invitation to *(mention any special summer activities or groups)*. Happy summer to you all.

Group 1: From baddy to goody – the good Samaritan (10 minutes)

Helpers should read the story beforehand in Luke 10.25-37.

Materials required Pens, labels, colour-by-letters worksheets, large picture of the good Samaritan, hobby horse (optional), bandages, money bag, eight photocopies of the play in plastic wallets or on card, five baseball hats – labelled 'Priest', 'Teacher', 'Samaritan', 'Innkeeper' and 'Jesus' (optional).

Visual focus Large picture of the good Samaritan.

With the first group, make a name badge – just their first name, written clearly – and write their full name on a worksheet.

Remember to keep ideas simple for Years 3 and 4, but expect more discussion with Years 5 and 6.

Helper *(Give out the scripts for the good Samaritan play and the labelled baseball hats, if using.)* We're going to act out the story of the good Samaritan as we read it. *(Hand out the parts. See page 102 for the script.)*

Jews think Samaritans are the baddies, their enemies. They have different religions and they hate one another. I wonder why Jesus makes a Samaritan the good guy in his story . . . *(To make us think about the story, about prejudice, how we think about and judge other people.)*

I wonder who our neighbour is . . . *(Anyone who needs our help.)*

What if they have a different religion? *(It doesn't matter.)*

What if they come from a different country? *(It doesn't matter.)*

What if we don't like them? *(It doesn't matter.)*

What if it costs us? *(It doesn't matter, we shouldn't expect anything in return.)*

I wonder if it's easy to be a good Samaritan, to care for people in need we don't even know or like, who may be different from us . . .

Helper **Activity**

Use a red pen to colour in the areas marked 'R' on your colour-by-letters worksheet. Listen or sing along to the *Neighbours* theme tune while colouring (optional).

Extra for Years 5 and 6 if needed

I wonder if you know any modern-day Samaritans . . . *(There is an organization called The Samaritans and you can ring if you are in trouble. The people who answer the phones will listen and try to help people, whatever they've done. Most charities help everyone, not just Christians – Christian Aid and the Red Cross, for example – and the Red Crescent helps everyone too, not just Muslims.)*

The good Samaritan

(You will need a narrator (this can be an adult or a child), a priest, teacher, Samaritan, innkeeper, Jesus, and all join in where it says 'Everyone'.)

Narrator   A lawyer tests Jesus. 'Teacher', he says, 'Who is my neighbour?' Jesus tells this story. A man going from Jerusalem to Jericho is attacked by robbers. They beat him, rob him and leave him half dead.

Everyone   Oh no!

Narrator   Look! There's a priest coming along the road. Surely he'll help the wounded man.

Priest   I can't help you, I might get blood on my hands.

Everyone   Oh no! The priest walks on by.

Narrator   Next comes a teacher. Maybe he'll/she'll help the wounded man.

Teacher   I can't help you, I'll be late for work.

Everyone   Oh no! The teacher walks on by.

Narrator   Now here's a foreigner from Samaria, an enemy of the Jews. Surely he'll walk past too, but . . .

Samaritan   You poor man, you need help. I'll look after you.

Narrator   The Samaritan bandages the man's wounds *(use bandages)*, puts him on his donkey *(use hobby horse, if available)*, takes him to an inn and pays the innkeeper *(hand over money bag)* to look after him.

Innkeeper   Thanks for the money. I'll look after this man until you come back.

Jesus   Which of these is a neighbour to the man who's been robbed?

Everyone   The one who looks after him. The good Samaritan.

Jesus   God wants us to be good Samaritans too.

I wonder how you feel about the story. Is there anything you want to say or ask about it? We may not have the answers, but we'll note down your questions. Some things about God are hard to understand.

Group 2: From sick to well – Jesus heals ten lepers (10 minutes)

Helpers should read the story beforehand in Luke 17.11–19.

Materials required   Pens, labels, colour-by-letters worksheets, people outline cards (laminated), washable pens, wipes, feel good and feel bad cards (A5 cards, laminated, to include a picture of flowers, fruit, medicine, praying hands, a sport, cake, wine, pet, sad face with words 'I'm all alone' and a TV), bandages, trellis cross.

Visual focus   Laid out on a small table or the floor, the feel good and feel bad cards by the trellis cross.

With the first group, make a name badge – just their first name, written clearly – and write their full name on a worksheet.

Remember to keep ideas simple for Years 3 and 4, but expect more discussion with Years 5 and 6.

Helper   *(Give out the feel good and feel bad cards.)* I wonder which pile you would put each of these cards in – the 'feel good' or 'feel bad' pile.

(Give everyone a people outline card, washable pen and a wipe.) We're going to use these cards to tell a story.

One day, ten lepers came to Jesus. I wonder what a leper is . . . *(It's a terrible disease, the hands and feet get very sore.)* Put spots on your people cards, especially on the hands, feet and face . . .

The ten lepers call out to Jesus and ask him to help them. I wonder what Jesus does . . . *(Jesus makes them well, their terrible disease disappears.)* So now you can wipe the spots off your cards.

I wonder what the lepers do now they're well . . . *(Get ideas – they go home, say thank you, celebrate . . . then go on with the story.)*

One of the lepers praises God and kneels at Jesus' feet to thank him. He's a Samaritan. I wonder who the Samaritans were . . . *(Someone from Samaria, a foreigner, not a Jew, the Jews' enemies.)* Jesus says, 'Ten lepers were healed. Where are the other nine? Has only one foreigner come back to praise God?' Jesus tells the Samaritan to go home; his faith has made him well.

The lepers come to Jesus to ask him to make them well. We can't come to Jesus like that now, but we can ask Jesus to help people who are sick or in trouble in our prayers. I wonder if you ask God to help people, if you pray for people . . .

I wonder if your prayers are answered . . .

Prayer is complicated. It's not like a shopping list! We can't tell God what to do. Only God knows what is best for each person. Sometimes the people we pray for get better, sometimes they don't. Everyone dies one day. God cares for everyone. Christians believe that God helps us with all our problems. God gives us peace, hope, courage and patience to live well. God works through doctors and nurses and medicine as well as prayer.

God wants *us* to help people too. I wonder how we can help people who are sick . . . We can get ideas from the feel good cards we sorted earlier . . . *(Give medicine, get a doctor, visit them, phone, send cards or flowers or gifts to show we care.)* We can make people feel better by being with them. We can give money to charities that help others. God can use all of us to make people feel better.

Helper

Activity 1

If you want, you can write the name of someone who needs help on a bandage and tie it on to the trellis cross to leave in church – we will pray to God and ask him to help them.

Helper

Activity 2

Use a blue pen to colour the areas marked 'B' on your colour-by-letters worksheet.

Extra for Years 5 and 6 if needed

I wonder who are like lepers today – people who are ignored or left out at school, in our community . . . *(People with HIV & AIDS, disabilities, those who are mentally ill, elderly, people who are different in some way.)* I wonder what we can do to help them . . .

I wonder how you feel about the story. Is there anything you want to say or ask about it? We may not have the answers, but we'll note down your questions. Some things about God are hard to understand.

Group 3: From small to big – Jesus feeds the five thousand (10 minutes)

Helpers should read the story beforehand in Mark 6.30-44 and John 6.1-13.

Materials required Pens, labels, colour-by-letters worksheets, picture of the feeding of the five thousand, Christian Aid or other charity posters, picture of or toy chicken, box of eggs.

Visual focus Picture of the feeding of the five thousand and the Christian Aid or other posters.

With the first group, make a name badge – just their first name, written clearly – and write their full name on a worksheet.

Remember to keep ideas simple for Years 3 and 4, but expect more discussion with Years 5 and 6.

Helper *(Show the picture of Jesus feeding the five thousand.)* I wonder if you know the story . . . *(Piece together the story and include that Jesus is teaching a crowd of five thousand men plus women and children. When the evening comes, they are hungry and the disciples want to send them away, but Jesus tells the disciples to give them something to eat. A little boy has five loaves and two fish. Jesus takes the bread and fish, thanks God and gives them to the crowd. Everyone has enough to eat and the disciples collect twelve baskets of leftover food. It's a miracle. It shows Jesus is God with us.)*

I wonder how Jesus changes five loaves and two fish into enough food for five thousand men plus women and children with twelve baskets of food left over . . . *(Let them say what they think. Bring out the observation that different people have different ideas about Jesus' miracles.[18] Some people take miracle stories literally – Jesus makes more food. Some people think that Jesus helps people share so there's enough food for everyone. We don't know how it happened, but we know what the story means. The story teaches us that everyone can make a difference. If we are willing to help, if we share what we have, like the little boy, God is able to use it.)*

God doesn't want people to be hungry. Jesus feeds the hungry. Charities like Christian Aid do this too. *(Show the picture of or toy chicken and box of eggs.)* I wonder what happens if you give a poor family a few chickens . . . *(They get eggs to eat, eggs to sell, chickens to eat, spare chickens to sell, chicken poo/manure to improve their crops.)*

Something as simple as a few chickens or goats, pigs or seeds makes a real difference to the millions of poor people in the world. It helps stop them being hungry and poor. There is enough food in the world if people with plenty share with the poor and help feed the hungry. Charities like Oxfam and Christian Aid make it easy for us to help. I wonder if you know about alternative presents for Christmas or Mother's Day or Easter . . . *(Instead of buying your friends and relatives things that they don't really need, you could spend the money instead on chickens, for example, or a toilet or funding for a teacher. Your family and friends would get cards of explanation and thanks from the charities concerned, and people in real need would benefit.)* I wonder what you think of this . . .

Helper	**Activity**
	Use a yellow pen to colour the areas marked 'Y' on your colour-by-letters worksheet. I wonder how you feel about the story. Is there anything you want to say or ask about it? We may not have the answers, but we'll note down your questions. Some things about God are hard to understand.

Group 4: From enemy to friend – Jesus meets Zacchaeus (10 minutes)

Helpers should read the story beforehand in Luke 19.1–10.

Materials required	Pens, labels, colour-by-letters worksheets, large picture of Zacchaeus, jar marked 'Romans', jar marked 'Me', effervescent vitamin tablets and four big test tubes with some water in them, small table, 30 wrapped sweets.
Visual focus	Large picture of Zacchaeus.
	With the first group, make a name badge – just their first name, written clearly – and write their full name on a worksheet.
	Remember to keep ideas simple for Years 3 and 4, but expect more discussion with Years 5 and 6.
Helper	*(Put the small table in the middle of the area for Group 4, with a chair and the two jars on the table.)* In Jesus' day, the Jews had to pay taxes to the Roman governor. Zacchaeus collects taxes for the Romans and keeps some for himself too. He's very rich. Who wants to be Zacchaeus? You can sit at this tax table.

(Give out a sweet to everyone.) It's not to eat now – you've got to give it to Zacchaeus, the tax collector, then you can sit down again. Zacchaeus, can you put some sweets in the pot marked 'Romans' and some sweets in the pot marked 'Me', please.

I wonder how you feel about Zacchaeus . . . *(No one likes Zacchaeus because he works for the Romans and keeps money for himself.)* Zacchaeus has no friends. He's not a happy man.

One day, Jesus comes to town. Zacchaeus climbs a sycamore tree to see Jesus because he's not very tall and there's a big crowd *(show large picture of Zacchaeus)*. Jesus sees

Zacchaeus in the tree and tells him to come down. Jesus asks to be his friend and stay in his house. I wonder what Zacchaeus thinks of this . . . (Surprised, happy.) Zacchaeus is so pleased Jesus is his friend that he gives half his money to the poor and promises to pay people back four times what he's taken from them. You'll get a sweet back at the end too!

Zacchaeus' life changes when he meets Jesus. Let's do a before and after picture . . .

Friends? Before, Zacchaeus has no friends. After, Jesus and the disciples are his friends.

Happiness? Before, Zacchaeus is unhappy. After, he's very happy.

Character? Before, Zacchaeus helps himself. After, he helps the poor. Before, he's a crook. After, he's honest.

Wealth? Before, Zacchaeus is rich. After, he's poor in money, rich in life.

I wonder if Zacchaeus is better before or after meeting Jesus . . .

Jesus changes Zacchaeus, like a vitamin tablet changes when you put it in water – see what happens . . . (drop a vitamin tablet into the water in one of the test tubes). It goes fizzy. Christians believe that Jesus changes us too. Jesus puts 'fizz' into our lives, he shows us how to be really happy, that what matters is to care and share.

Helper

Activity

Use a green pen to colour the areas marked 'G' on your colour-by-letters worksheet. I wonder how you feel about the story. Is there anything you want to say or ask about it? We may not have the answers, but we'll note down your questions. Some things about God are hard to understand.

Workshop 4: Who is Jesus?

Overview of workshop   See the at-a-glance summary, page 118.

You will need
- Timer.
- CD player.
- CD of music (such as Taizé, Celtic, worship songs, spirituals) or CD of optional song, one verse of 'Put your hand in the hand of the man who stilled the waters'.[19]

For each class of 30: felt-tip pens, sticky labels, invitations on A5 paper or thin card, words 'storyteller', 'healer', 'miracle-maker' and 'friend' printed out on thin card and laminated, plus the name 'Jesus' printed out four times to make four thin laminated cards, large pictures of the sower, paralysed man, Jesus calming the storm, Jesus calling the disciples (Turvey[20] or other), hats for a teacher, nurse, wizard and fool, 'crown of thorns',[21] crown, 30 fizzy fish sweets.

For Group 1: six baseball hats (labelled with pictures of the sun, a bird's beak and four labelled with pictures of seeds), a thorn hula-hoop (with paper spikes).

For Group 2: bottles of medicine, including sore throat lozenges, big Jenga or other building bricks, army action figure toy, rectangular mat (large enough to accommodate toy figure lying down) with a string attached to each corner.

For Group 3: parachute or blue sheet, small toy boat.

For Group 4: small paper fishes, large net, short pieces of wool, story of Jesus calling his disciples (Mark 1.16-20, see below) printed out and laminated.

Preparation Play the CD of songs as the children come in and leave. Set up four small-group areas with the visual focus as indicated in the materials for each group (see below). Photocopy the notes for the helpers and gather together all the other materials required.

Craft Photocopy an invitation to church activities (see invitation template, Chapter 10). On the blank back of the invitation, the children draw around one hand and copy the word for each activity on to a finger and palm (see example template, Chapter 10). There is space to include the address of the church website (and joint town churches' website), if available, to help parents and children follow up the experience in church.

Leader ### Introduction to each session (5 minutes)

(Welcome the children at the church door and lead them to the pews or seats at the front of the church. Invite them to put their coats and so on under the pews or seats to be collected at the end of the session.)

Welcome to our 'Who is Jesus?' workshop. Have you ever wondered what God is like . . . ? Jesus says that if we know him, we know God. Jesus shows us what God is like. I wonder what we know about Jesus? What is he like? What does he do . . . ? *(Let the children answer, but don't comment or add ideas. They may say Jesus heals people, tells stories, does miracles, makes friends, is kind, loving, forgiving, welcoming.)*

We'll see what else you can find out as you go round the groups today.

Your teacher will put you into four small groups to go round each activity. The buzzer will tell us when to change.

You'll be given a sticky label to write your name on, so we know who you are – just your first name as clearly as you can. The team members have their labels on already – let me introduce them to you now . . . You'll also be given a piece of paper and we'll ask you to draw round your hand and add a word and picture to your fingers in each of the four activities, plus words for your thumb and palm. We hope you'll show people at home your special hand and tell them what you did in church today.

Leader ### Conclusion to each session (15 minutes)

Let's see what you found out today about Jesus. Use the hands you've made to help you.

- *(Jesus is a storyteller, his stories teach us about God.*
- *Jesus is a healer, he makes people well.*
- *Jesus is a miracle maker, he changes lives.*
- *Jesus is a friend – he wants us to be his friend, to be like him.*
- *Jesus is special – he is God with us.)*

These hats remind us of Jesus too. *(Put the hats on helpers at the front and go through them.)*

- Teacher's hat – Jesus teaches us.
- Nurse's hat – Jesus makes people well, on the inside and outside.
- Wizard's hat – Jesus changes lives, but by miracles, not magic.
- Fool's hat – Jesus is our friend even when it would seem foolish to people, and some people think Jesus is a fool because he dies on the cross for us.

Two more hats tell us why Jesus is special.

- Crown of thorns – Jesus dies on the cross.
- King's crown – Jesus rises to new life, he's the king of kings, the king of glory.

We're going to end with a clapping rhyme. We'll show you, then you can do it too. You need to stand up and face a partner.

These are my hands *(clap hands together, then with partner, two times)*.
Hands for healing *(pat partner on the shoulder, four times)*.
These are my hands *(clap hands together, then with partner, two times)*.
Hands of peace *(make peace sign with fingers)*.
These are my hands *(clap hands together, then with partner, two times)*.
Hands tell a story *(make book shape with hands and open)*.
These are my hands *(clap hands together, then with partner, two times)*.
Be friends please *(shake hands, four times)*.

(Ask helpers for any interesting questions or comments.)

*(**Optional song**: one verse of 'Put your hand in the hand of the man who stilled the waters'.)*

Thank you for working so well today. We'll leave the fishing net with your names on in church so the congregation on Sunday can see what you have been doing with us. Enjoy your fizzy fish sweet when your teacher says you can eat it. Don't forget your invitation to *(mention any special summer activities or groups here, as appropriate)*. A happy summer to you all.

Group 1: Jesus the storyteller - the parable of the sower (10 minutes)

Helpers should read the story beforehand in Mark 4.1-20.

Materials required   Pens, labels, sheet of A5 paper or thin card with invitation on back, six baseball hats (labelled with pictures of the sun, a bird's beak and four labelled with pictures of seeds), a thorn hula-hoop (with paper spikes), large picture of the sower, words 'Storyteller' and 'Jesus' printed out on card and laminated.

Visual focus   Large picture of the sower and word 'storyteller'.

With the first group, make a name badge - just their first name, written clearly - and write their full name on their sheet of paper or thin card with the invitation on the back.

Remember to keep ideas simple for Years 3 and 4, but expect more discussion with Years 5 and 6.

Helper   We're going to act out one of Jesus' stories - the story of the sower. *(Show the large picture of the sower. Give out the hats and props as follows.)* We need a bird. *(Place the baseball hat with a bird's beak picture on a child and put him or her in one corner.)*

We need the sun. *(Place the baseball hat with the sun picture on a child and put him or her in another corner.)*

We need a thorn. *(Give the thorn hoop-la to a child and put him or her in another corner.)*

We need seeds. The rest of you are seeds. *(Give out the four baseball hats with the seed pictures and place those wearing them in the remaining corner.)*

Jesus tells the story of the sower to a crowd of people. I'm going to be the sower. You all listen carefully, ready to act your parts.

A sower goes out to sow *(pretend to scatter seed)*. As he sows, some seed falls on the path. *(Guide one seed to the bird's beak corner.)* I wonder what happens to this seed on the path . . . You're right - the bird gobbles it up *(move the seed behind the bird, out of sight)*.

Some seed falls on rocky ground *(guide one seed to the sun corner).* This seed starts to grow *(ask the seed to stretch up).* It has no roots. I wonder what happens to this seed . . . You're right – the hot sun burns it and it withers away *(ask seed to fall down).*

Some seed falls in the thorns *(guide a seed to the thorn corner).* I wonder what happens to this seed . . . You're right – it starts to grow *(tell seed to stretch up),* but the thorns choke it – *(ask child to put hoop over the seed and the seed to fall down).*

Some seed lands on good soil *(point to the seed left in the last corner).* I wonder what happens to this seed . . . You're right – it grows and grows *(ask the seed to stretch up and up)* and produces lots of other seeds.

Let's all sit in a circle now and think about what Jesus' story means.

I wonder who the sower is . . . *(Jesus, anyone who tells us about God).*

I wonder who the seeds are . . . *(anyone who hears about God).*

Some people hear about God and aren't bothered, like birds gobbling up the seed. That's you – the first seed.

Other people follow Jesus, but when trouble comes, like the hot sun, they forget about God, like the seed on the rocky ground. That's you – the second seed.

Some people follow Jesus, but money or work or play get in the way. Like thorns, these other things take over so there's no room for God. That's you – the third seed.

Some seed falls on good soil. That's people who hear about God and want to be like Jesus. That's you – the fourth seed.

Helper | **Activity**

I wonder which seed in the story you want to be . . . You can think about that as you draw round your hand. Write 'storyteller' on one of the fingers. Draw some seeds or something to remind you of the story. (**Note**: *If this is the children's fourth activity, ask them also to add the word 'Jesus' to the thumb and 'God with us' to the palm.)*

Is there anything you want to say or ask about the story? We may not have the answers, but we'll note down your questions. Some things about God are hard to understand.

Group 2: Jesus the healer – the paralysed man (10 minutes)

Helpers should read the story beforehand in Mark 2.1-12.

Materials required | Pens, labels, sheet of A5 paper or thin card with invitation on back, bottles of medicine, including sore throat lozenges, big Jenga or other building bricks, army action figure toy, mat with four strings, large picture of the paralysed man, word 'Healer' printed out on card and laminated.

Visual focus | Large picture of paralysed man and word 'Healer'.

With the first group, make a name badge – just their first name, written clearly – and write their full name on their sheet of paper or thin card with the invitation on the back.

Remember to keep ideas simple for Years 3 and 4, but expect more discussion with Years 5 and 6.

Helper | If you've got a sore throat, how could your mum or dad help you? *(Give you sore throat lozenges. Show them.)* I've got other medicines with me too – medicines for headaches, allergies, tummy ache, colds *(show).*

What if you couldn't move, if you were paralysed? Is there a medicine that could make you get up and walk again? *(No.)*

(Show large picture of paralysed man.) I wonder if any of you know this story . . . Let's use these props to piece together what happens.

One day, Jesus is teaching in a house full of people. Can you build me the house with these bricks . . . Four friends decide to bring their paralysed friend to Jesus. They carry him on a mat with strings tied to it. They believe Jesus can help their paralysed friend, but there's a problem – they can't get into the house, there are too many people . . . *(give the army action figure toy on the mat with strings to a child)*. I wonder what the friends do now . . . maybe they give up and go home or maybe they make a hole in the roof above Jesus . . . *(ask a child to take off the roof)* and lower their friend down through the hole on his mat, so he's right in front of Jesus . . . *(do this with the action figure on the mat)*.

I wonder what Jesus does now . . . Jesus makes this man well on the inside and on the outside. First, Jesus forgives the things he's done wrong, so the man feels better inside. Then Jesus tells him to get up, take up his mat and go home. The man does as Jesus says, as he's healed inside and outside too. *(Stand the action figure up.)* It's a miracle. The crowd praises God. God heals through Jesus. Jesus is God with us.

Let's think about the story together. The four men bring their friend on a mat to Jesus. We can't bring people to Jesus like that now, but we can ask Jesus to help people who are sick or in trouble in our prayers. I wonder if you pray for people . . .

We can't tell God what to do. Only God knows what is best for each person. I wonder if God always heals our bodies . . . *(No.)* Sometimes the people we pray for get better, sometimes they don't. Our bodies wear out. Everyone dies one day, but God cares for everyone. Christians believe that God helps us deal with our problems. He gives us peace and hope.

I wonder if God always make us better on the inside . . . *(Yes.)* When we ask him, God always forgives us and puts us right inside.

There are lots of stories about Jesus healing people. I wonder if you can heal people too . . . This may surprise you, but we all have the power to heal. Have you seen someone crying or feeling sad? You can ask what's the matter, listen to them, maybe give them a hug or do something to help. We make people feel better by being with them, doing what we can.

Extra for Years 5 and 6 if needed

Sometimes people look OK on the outside, but they are worried, afraid, shy, lonely or sad inside, they feel bad about how they look or have problems at home or school. We can't always see what's wrong from the outside. I wonder if you know what I mean . . . Christians believe that God makes a difference inside. God loves us as we are – God has no favourites; everyone is special to God.

Helper

Activity

Write 'healer' on a finger of your paper hand. Draw some bricks or something from the story. (**Note:** *If this is the children's fourth activity, ask them also to add the word 'Jesus' to the thumb and 'God with us' to the palm.*)

Is there anything you want to say or ask about the story? We may not have the answers, but we'll note down your questions. Some things about God are hard to understand.

Group 3: Jesus the miracle-maker – calming the storm (10 minutes)

Helpers should read the story beforehand in Mark 4.35–41.

Materials required   Pens, labels, sheet of A5 paper or thin card with invitation on back, parachute or blue sheet, small toy boat, large picture of Jesus calming the storm, words 'Miracle-maker' and 'Jesus' printed out on card and laminated.

Visual focus   Large picture of Jesus calming the storm and word 'Miracle-maker'.

With the first group, make a name badge – just their first name, written clearly – and write their full name on their sheet of paper or thin card with the invitation on the back.

Remember to keep ideas simple for Years 3 and 4, but expect more discussion with Years 5 and 6.

Helper   I wonder if you've been in a bad storm . . . One day, Jesus and his friends are caught in a storm on the Sea of Galilee *(show picture)*. We're going to act out this story with a parachute/ sheet. You'll need to stand in a circle and hold on to the parachute/sheet. Don't move it yet. Wait for the story. *(Hold out the parachute/sheet, put the small boat in the middle).*

One day, Jesus and his friends go out in a boat on the Sea of Galilee. At first, the sea is calm and still. Jesus falls asleep on the boat. Then a wind begins to blow, gently. *(Start lifting the parachute up and down gently.)*

The wind gets a little stronger and the boat rocks about, but Jesus still sleeps. *(Lift the parachute/sheet up and down a bit more.)*

Then the waves get really big. *(Lift the parachute/sheet up and down a lot.)* The sky flashes with lightning, thunder cracks, rain is pouring down. It's a terrible storm! Jesus' friends wake him up. 'Help!' they cry. 'We're going to drown.' Jesus wakes up. Jesus says to the wind and the waves, 'Peace, be still.' The wind and the waves stop. All is calm again. *(Stop moving the parachute/sheet.)*

It's a miracle – a sign that Jesus has the power to help us. Jesus is God with us.

Now we're going to lift the parachute/sheet up and sit underneath it together to think about the story and what it means. *(Ask a few of the children to hold the sheet up while the rest sit under it with the helper(s).)*

I wonder if we have storms in our lives, times when we're frightened or upset, when things go wrong . . . Life isn't always easy and sometimes difficult things happen – arguments with parents or brothers and sisters, things we're afraid of, problems we face. They're like a big storm – like winds and waves that toss us about – but Jesus is with his friends in the storm, ready to help them when they ask him.

We can't see God, but Christians believe that God is always with us, ready to help us when we ask him. When we feel sad or afraid or angry, we can talk to God and ask for his help.

I wonder how God helps us . . . *(God calms us, helps us deal with anger, sadness and fear, to see what really matters, find the loving, forgiving way.)*

Helper   **Activity 1**

We're going to be quiet under the parachute and think about things that make us sad or angry or afraid. If you want, you can ask God to help you and give you his peace.

Helper   **Activity 2**

(Come out from under the parachute/sheet.) Write 'miracle-maker' on a finger of your paper hand. Draw a wave or anything that reminds you of the story. (**Note**: If this is the

children's fourth activity, ask them also to add the word 'Jesus' to the thumb and 'God with us' to the palm.)

Extra for Years 5 and 6 if needed

Calming the storm is a miracle. A miracle isn't magic - it's God's power helping us.

I wonder what you think about miracles ... Some people take miracle stories literally - they think Jesus actually makes the sea calm. Some other people think that Jesus just calms his friends' fears. We don't know for sure what happened, but we know what's important - the story tells us that Jesus and God are with us and can help us whatever happens.

Is there anything you want to say or ask about the story? We may not have the answers, but we'll note down your questions. Some things about God are hard to understand.

Group 4: Jesus the friend (10 minutes)

Helpers should read the story beforehand in Mark 1.16-20.

Materials required   Pens, labels, sheet of A5 paper or thin card with invitation on back, small paper fishes, large net, short pieces of wool, large picture of Jesus calling the disciples, words 'Friend' and 'Jesus' printed out on card and laminated, story of Jesus calling his disciples (Mark 1.16-20, see below) printed out and laminated.

Visual focus   Large picture of Jesus calling the disciples and the words 'Friend' and 'Jesus'.

With the first group, make a name badge - just their first name, written clearly - and write their full name on their sheet of paper or thin card with the invitation on the back.

Remember to keep ideas simple for Years 3 and 4, but expect more discussion with Years 5 and 6.

Helper   I wonder if you know how to play Follow my leader ... *(Let the children explain, then summarize.)* One person's the leader, everyone lines up behind that person and does what the leader does. Let's have a quick game. Who wants to be the leader ... ?

I wonder if you know the game Trust ... *(Let the children explain and then summarize.)* You ask someone to do something scary because they trust you - for example, you say, 'Fall back and I'll catch you'. If they trust you, they'll do what you say. Don't look worried, we're not going to do that today! We're going to see if Jesus' friends trust him enough to do what he tells them and follow him. Would anyone like to read the story ... ? *(This is a story based on Mark 1.16-20, The Message.)*

Jesus calls the disciples

Passing along the beach of Lake Galilee, Jesus saw Simon and his brother Andrew net-fishing. Fishing was their regular work. Jesus said to them, 'Come with me. I'll make a new kind of fisherman out of you. I'll show you how to catch men and women instead of perch and bass.' They didn't ask questions. They dropped their nets and followed.

A dozen yards or so down the beach he saw the brothers James and John, Zebedee's sons. They were in the boat mending their fishnets. Right off, he made the same offer. Immediately, they left their father Zebedee, the boat, and the hired hands, and followed.

I wonder why James, John, Simon and Andrew decide to follow Jesus . . . *(He's exciting, different, it's an adventure, they like Jesus, Jesus is special, they trust him.)*

I wonder if you would have followed Jesus, like James, John, Simon and Andrew . . .

It would have been risky, meant leaving a safe job, leaving home and family, a lot to give up!

I wonder why Christians follow Jesus today . . . *(Jesus is special, God with us, brings out the best in us, teaches us how to treat other people and the world we live in, helps us live well even when times are hard.)*

I wonder why some people don't follow Jesus today . . . *(Don't believe in him or in God, don't want to think about or help other people.)*

Extra for Years 5 and 6 if needed

I wonder what Jesus means by 'fishing for people' . . . *(Jesus asks his friends to share his work, telling people about God, making people well, loving people.)*

Jesus asks people to follow him – not just the disciples long ago, but people today too, all of us. We can decide for ourselves if we want to follow Jesus – it's our choice and no one can decide for us.

Helper

Activity 1

You can write your name on a paper fish and tie it to the net with a piece of wool to show you are Jesus' friends and want to be like him.

Helper

Activity 2

Write 'friend' on a finger of your paper hand and draw a fish or something to remind you of the story. (**Note**: *If this is the children's fourth activity, ask them also to add the word 'Jesus' to the thumb and 'God with us' to the palm.)*

Is there anything you want to say or ask about the story? We may not have the answers, but we'll note down your questions. Some things about God are hard to understand.

8
At-a-glance summaries

1 Christmas workshops

Year cycle	Theme	To take away	Display in church	Group 1	Group 2	Group 3	Group 4	Summary/ optional song
Year 1	Christmas animals	Card with invitation and small chocolate	Nativity figures in Christmas decorations and explanation	Journey to Bethlehem Donkey: patient and willing (Luke 2.1-5)	Born in a stable Rat: being content (Luke 2.6-7)	Shepherds hear the news Sheep: generous and giving (Luke 2.8-20)	Wise men journey Camel: keep going Good and bad in all (Matthew 2.1-18)	Jesus is the reason for the season Sing 'Super Duper Christmas'
Year 2	Christmas angels	Angel and invitation with text (Luke 2.10), small chocolate	Large angel and explanation	Mary - 'yes' to God Cut out angel (Luke 1.26-38)	Joseph - seeing differently Stick on wings (Matthew 1.18-25)	Shepherds - sharing good news Stick on halo (Luke 2.8-20)	Wise men - get it wrong, put it right Decorate angel with stars (Matthew 2.1-18)	Listening to angels - it's your choice Sing 'Here we go up to Bethlehem'
Year 3	Christmas gifts	Wise men card with invitation, small chocolate	Pictures of Jesus and explanation	Gold for a king - what kind of king? Nativity picture (Matthew 2.1-12)	Frankincense for God - what is God like? Pictures of Jesus (Matthew 2.1-12)	Myrrh for burial - sad times Scented candles (Matthew 2.1-12)	Looking for Jesus - not what you expect (Matthew 2.1-12)	Christmas trees, wise men, Easter Our gifts to Jesus Sing 'The Little Drummer Boy' or 'We Three Kings'
Year 4	Help! It's Christmas	Card with pictures, invitation and text (John 3.16), small hard sweets	Paper chain 'Thank you' box and explanation	Journey to Bethlehem - refugees Links in a chain Sand on card (Luke 2.1-5; Matthew 2.13-15)	The innkeeper makes room - being homeless 'Thank you' box Straw on card (Luke 2.6-7)	Shepherds - not left out Wrapping sweets Cotton wool on cards (Luke 2.8-20)	Wise men - sharing our gifts Gift tag Star on card (Matthew 2.1-12)	Doing what we can - starfish story Sing 'We wish you a Merry Christmas'

2 Easter workshops

Year cycle	Theme	To take away	Display in church	Group 1	Group 2	Group 3	Group 4	Summary/ optional song
Year 1	Easter footprints	Easter spinner with invitation, mini egg with explanation	Footprints – 'Love and serve'	Palm Sunday – the donkey Palm Sunday play Donkey footprint (Matthew 21.1-11)	Maundy Thursday – foot washing Foot printing and washing Human footprint (John 13.2-17)	Good Friday – the cockerel Peter's choices quiz Cockerel footprint (Matthew 26.69-75)	Easter Day – butterfly Clean coin Story with props Butterfly (Matthew 28.1-9)	'Putting it right', a new start for Peter and us
Year 2	Easter words	Mini Easter garden in dish with invitation and text (John 12.24), mini egg with explanation	Large Easter garden	Palm Sunday – hope Story with stones Palm sticker (Luke 19.28-40)	The Last Supper – love Foil cup and plate (Mark 14.22-23)	The cross – forgiveness Jesus dies on the cross play Straw cross (Luke 23)	Resurrection – new life Story with bulb Flower on cocktail stick, dough tomb, stone (John 20.1-20)	Words for Easter Add JOY Flower cross Sing 'Celebrate'
Year 3	Easter friends	Hot cross bun card and invitation with text (John 15.12), mini egg with explanation	Trellis cross and wool ties – 'I'll be there for you'	Going with the crowd Friendship quiz (John 12.12-19, 19.4-16)	A meal to remember Last Supper figures (Luke 22.14-20; I Corinthians 11.23-25)	I'll be there for you Taizé cross Tie wool on to trellis cross (John 19.16-19, 25-30)	A friend for ever Mary and Thomas meet Jesus Relighting candle (John 20.1-18, 24-29)	Coconut summary Friends theme tune
Year 4	Eggy Easter	Easter Egg card with invitation and text (John 15.13), mini egg with explanation	Eggs in egg boxes and sticky note headlines on 4 boards	Hosanna Open eggs to tell story Kings and crowds (Mark 11.1-11)	Remember me Open eggs to tell story Judas – being sorry (Matthew 26.26-30)	Father forgive Open eggs to tell story Joseph, soldiers, forgiving (Luke 23.26-43)	He is risen Open eggs to tell story Resurrection play: the empty tomb (Luke 24.1-12)	Importance of Easter Years 5 and 6 headlines Sing 'Lord, I lift your name on high'

3 Jesus workshops

Year cycle	Theme	To take away	Display in church	Group 1	Group 2	Group 3	Group 4	Summary/ optional song
Year 1	Jesus' special prayer	Paper game, invitation with Lord's Prayer, fizzy fish	Large-text version of Lord's Prayer, game and explanation	Our Father in heaven, hallowed be your name Bread and stone props, dough Colour snake (Matthew 7.7-11)	Your will be done, on earth as in heaven Lost sheep with props Colour sheep (Luke 15.1-7)	Give us today our daily bread Building bigger barns play Colour bread (Luke 12.13-21)	Forgive us, as we forgive Unforgiving servant, Brick New Testament Forgiveness quiz (Matthew 18.21-35)	Lord's Prayer with actions Text version of Lord's Prayer Sing 'Lord's Prayer'
Year 2	Four faces of Jesus	Four faces on a cross with invitation and text (John 14.9), pig sweet	Pill sticky note prayers on medicine bottle board and explanation	Angry Jesus – who is the greatest? Famous people's faces Wool frown (Luke 9.46-48; Matthew 18.1-5; Mark 10.33-37)	Crying Jesus – healing Jairus' daughter Healing Jairus' daughter play Gel or glitter tears (Matthew 9.18-19, 23-26; Mark 5.22-24, 35-43; Luke 8.41-42, 49-56)	Laughing Jesus – the wedding at Cana Water to wine Googly eyes (John 2.1-11)	Loving Jesus – the prodigal Son Story with props Heart cheeks (Luke 15.11-32)	Like Jesus, like God – happy, sad angry and loving Sing 'Our God is a great big God'
Year 3	Jesus changes lives	Colour-by-letters sheet with invitation and text (John 10.10), wrapped sweets	Prayer bandages on trellis cross and explanation	Baddy to goody – the good Samaritan The good Samaritan play (Luke 10.25-37)	Sick to well – Jesus heals ten lepers Feel good/feel bad cards Prayer bandages on trellis cross (Luke 17.11-19)	Small to big – Jesus feeds the five thousand Christian Aid posters (Mark 6.30-44; John 6.1-13)	Enemy to friend – Jesus meets Zacchaeus Zacchaeus changes Make fizzy water (Luke 19.1-10)	Life in fullness Cloth made dirty and clean 'Meek and mild' pictures of Jesus Sing 'Hosanna'
Year 4	Who is Jesus?	Drawn hand, words and images with invitation and text (John 1.18), fizzy fish sweet	Fishing net, named fish and explanation	Jesus the storyteller – parable of the sower Act story Draw seeds (Mark 4.1-20)	Jesus the healer – the paralysed man Tell story with props Draw bricks (Mark 2.1-12)	Jesus the miracle-maker – calming the storm Tell story with parachute Draw a wave (Mark 4.35-41)	Jesus the friend Calls fishermen Tie fish on to net Names on fish (Mark 1.16-20)	Jesus shows us what God is like Hats summary Clapping rhyme Sing 'Put your hand in the hand of the man who stilled the waters'

9
Handouts

Notes for RE Active Church helpers

Thank you for being part of the RE Active Church team. This valuable work with schools could not happen without you. Don't worry: you don't have to be an expert theologian! Like every Christian, you are called to model Jesus to others, to be Christ to others, to be *Christlike*.

Before each session

- Please pray for the schools, children and staff and the RE Active Church team.
- Read and reflect on the Bible passage to be used in your small group.
- Get to know the ten minutes of material for your small group. Flag up any issues.
  (*Note:* You don't have to memorize it – a copy is provided.)
- Read through the aims and remit of RE Active Church (below).
- New helpers shadow a group before running a small group on their own.
- Everything you need for your session will be provided.

Aims and remit of RE Active Church

We aim to serve local schools by contributing to the RE and general school curriculum in ways that support teachers and enhance children's educational experiences.

We aim to help children explore the relationship between the Christian story and their own lives. We contribute to children's spiritual nurture and general development, promoting awareness of self and of others, empathy and communication skills.

We do not aim to convert the children. Instead, we assist schools in an area that many teachers find daunting, but of which we have personal understanding and experience.

We provide:

- multisensory material to engage children with different learning styles in active learning
- opportunities for wonder, creativity and fun
- a safe place for children to ask questions, express ideas and feelings, be listened to and listen to others
- we value process over product – what the children make does not have to be perfect; it's what they learn along the way that's important!

During each session

- Be welcoming and positive to each child.
- Be flexible in using material, sensing when to move on in an activity or discussion.
- Encourage, but do not force, everyone to participate. Facilitate children listening to each other – allow only one child to speak at a time.
- Listen carefully to children's questions and answers; affirm each child's contribution.

Helpful responses include, 'Mmm', 'That's interesting', 'I wonder what others think', 'That sounds difficult/good', 'I don't know, but I'll try to find out for you later', 'Christians don't have all the answers', 'lots of Christians struggle with this' . . . It is important to:

- respond simply to children's questions, making a note of any difficult questions;
- talk naturally and simply about your own faith experiences when appropriate, but not impose your views on others;
- expect the best from each child – alert the teacher or teaching assistant to any unacceptable behaviour, first-aid issues, a child needing to go to the toilet and so on.

After each session

Give feedback – what worked or didn't work well, any problems, ideas to improve the session.

We look forward to welcoming you to RE Active Church. Material for each workshop will be sent to the RE coordinator in your school ahead of your visit to church. Your feedback on the material is invited before and after each visit.

Aims of RE Active Church

We aim to serve local schools by contributing to the RE and general school curriculum in ways that support teachers and enhance children's educational experiences.

We aim to help children explore the relationship between the Christian story and their own lives, contributing to children's spiritual nurture and general development, promoting awareness of self and others, empathy and communication skills.

We do not aim to convert the children. Instead, we assist schools in an area that many teachers find daunting, but of which we have personal understanding and experience.

In partnership with the school, RE Active Church challenges the consumer-driven, materialistic, 'me first' celebrity culture and reinforces values taught by schools across the curriculum.

RE Active Church:

- provides multisensory material to engage children with different learning styles in active learning, prepared by Christians who are trained teachers
- encourages participation by using pictures, simple plays, quizzes, songs, acted stories, visual aids and artefacts, music, reflective silence and craft, with opportunities for wonder, creativity and fun
- invites, but does not force, children to respond
- provides a safe place for children to ask questions, express ideas and feelings, be listened to and listen to others.

We value process over product – the outcomes of the craft activities do not have to be perfect.

Before each session

Please carry out a risk assessment before your visit. RE Active Church is risk-aware in setting up the activities and low-risk because:

- health and safety issues are a compulsory part of church life;
- children are instructed to walk, not run, as they enter and leave the church and move from one small group activity to another;
- all craft activities are age-appropriate and supervised;
- any consumption of food or drink is agreed with the teacher.

The church group will provide everything needed for each workshop. Please divide each class into four small groups and let us know of any special needs. →

Each one-hour workshop is divided into six parts:

- a five-minute introduction to the whole class at the front of the church;
- four ten-minute small group activities in different parts of the church;
- a fifteen-minute plenary concluding session for the whole class at the front of the church;
- each child makes a name label in their first small group activity;
- each child works on making something to take away;
- each child is given a small sweet as they leave with the provisos that:
  - an alternative sweet is offered in case of allergies;
  - teachers say when the children can eat the sweet - at the end of the workshop, at school, at home;
  - if requested, the sweets will be given to the teacher to distribute at the end of the school day rather than to the children as they leave the church.

Please try to keep to the time agreed for your workshop and let us know if there is a problem.

Contact (person X) on mobile number (00000 000000).

During each session

RE Active Church helpers are never alone with any child. The teacher is always responsible for the class, accompanied by a teaching assistant and/or parent helpers. It is the teacher's responsibility to take children to the toilet, administer first aid, sort out matters of discipline and count children in and out of church. We expect the best from each child. Helpers will alert the teacher or teaching assistant of any unacceptable behaviour, first-aid issues or if children need the toilet.

After each session

Please give feedback as to what worked well or did not work, and let us know of any problems or suggestions for improvement.

Sample rota

CHRISTMAS SCHOOL VISITS

Time and class	Group 1	Group 2	Group 3	Group 4	Additional helper
9.30 to 10.30 Yr?					
10.30 to 11.30 Yr?					
Lunch	Lunch	Lunch	Lunch	Lunch	Lunch
1.15 to 2.15 Yr?					
2.15 to 3.15 Yr?					

Date:

Name and phone no. of school:

Time and class	Group 1	Group 2	Group 3	Group 4	Additional helper
9.30 to 10.30 Yr?					
10.30 to 11.30 Yr?					
Lunch	Lunch	Lunch	Lunch	Lunch	Lunch
1.15 to 2.15 Yr?					
2.15 to 3.15 Yr?					

Date:

Name and phone no. of school:

A very big thank you for helping with this vital outreach work. As usual, there will be four small groups. Everything you need will be supplied in church. Notes about each session will be given to you before the workshop. If you have a problem with your allocated slots, please let me know asap (telephone . . .).

10
Craft templates

Instructions

The templates are designed to be photocopied, and sometimes the cards and games have to be cut out. Templates for Christmas Workshops 1, 3 and 4; Easter Workshops 1, 3 and 4; and Jesus Workshop 3 should be photocopied back to back, as indicated in the template headings. However, some of the templates require a little more explanation to use. Instructions for those are given below.

If you choose to increase the size of, for example, a card or invitation template, photocopying it at 120 per cent will enlarge it to fill an A4 sheet.

Cards for Christmas Workshop 1: Christmas animals and Workshop 4: Help! It's Christmas

1 Photocopy the picture template (Card template FRONT).

2 Photocopy the invitation template (Card template BACK) on the back of the picture template. The tops of both templates are as shown.

3 When the children have finished colouring in the card, fold the first fold back, so that the pictures are all on the outside and the invitation is hidden inside.

4 Fold the second fold, so that picture 1 is on the front, pictures 2 and 3 are inside, and picture 4 is on the back.

Spinner for Easter Workshop 1: Easter footprints

1 Photocopy the first picture template (Easter spinner template TOP).

2 Cut out the circle and the section indicated on the template.

3 On a separate piece of paper, photocopy the second picture template (Easter spinner template BOTTOM/FRONT).

4 Photocopy the invitation template (Easter spinner template BOTTOM/BACK) on the back of the second picture template.

5 Cut out the double-sided circle.

6 Carefully align the top circle (picture-side up) on the bottom circle (picture-side up).

7 Fasten them through the centre with a fastener or split pin, so that the top circle can rotate freely over the bottom one.

Paper game for Jesus Workshop 1: Jesus' special prayer

1 Fold the outermost triangular flaps backwards, along the folds marked 1.

2 Fold the next flaps inwards, along the folds marked 2, so that the words in the smallest square are covered.

3 Fold the square in half, to make a rectangle.

4 Fold the rectangle in half, to make a small square.

5 Unfold the square to make the rectangle again.

6 Push the tops of the pictures (the top corners) together to create a diamond and to reveal the flaps under which both thumbs and forefingers can be inserted.

Christmas - Workshop 1: Christmas animals
Card template FRONT

Christmas – Workshop 1: Christmas animals
Card template BACK

Peace on earth, good will to all people.

INSIDE SECOND FOLD

Happy Christmas

INSIDE FIRST FOLD

INSIDE FIRST FOLD

Name:

We'd love to see you at any of our Christmas services or events:

INSIDE SECOND FOLD

Christmas - Workshop 2: Christmas angels
Angel template

Christmas – Workshop 2: Christmas angels
Invitation template

'Do not be afraid ... I am bringing you good news of great joy for all people.'

Luke 2.10

We'd love to see you at any of our Christmas services or events:

'Do not be afraid ... I am bringing you good news of great joy for all people.'

Luke 2.10

We'd love to see you at any of our Christmas services or events:

Christmas - Workshop 2: Christmas angels

Maze templates: easy - top; harder - bottom

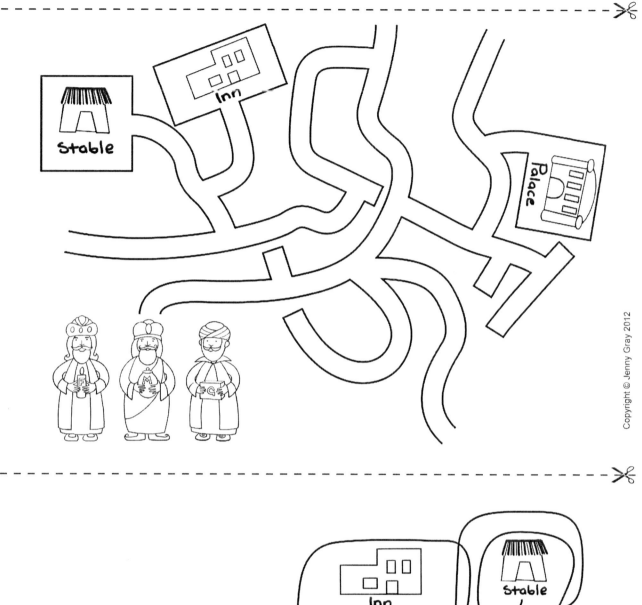

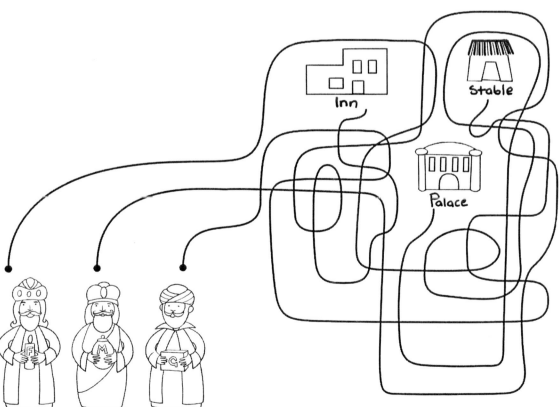

Christmas – Workshop 3: Christmas gifts
Wise men card template FRONT

We'd love to see you at any of our Christmas services or events:

FOLD

Christmas – Workshop 3: Christmas gifts
Wise men card template BACK

The wise men looked
for Jesus.
Wise men and women
seek him still.

- INSIDE FOLD -

May God bless you this
Christmas, with love from
everyone at

Christmas – Workshop 4: Help! It's Christmas
Card template FRONT

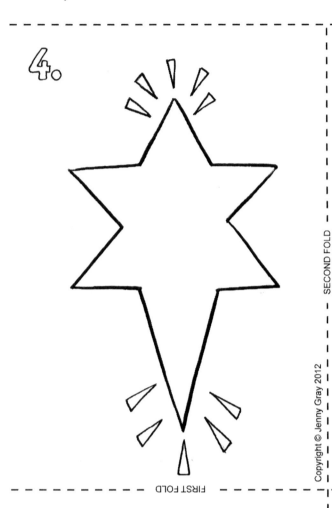

Christmas - Workshop 4: Help! It's Christmas
Card template BACK

'God so loved the world that he gave his only Son...'
John 3.16

Happy Christmas

INSIDE SECOND FOLD

INSIDE FIRST FOLD

INSIDE FIRST FOLD

Name:

We'd love to see you at any of our Christmas services or events:

INSIDE SECOND FOLD

Easter - Workshop 1: Easter footprints
Easter spinner template TOP

Easter - Workshop 1: Easter footprints
Easter spinner template BOTTOM/FRONT

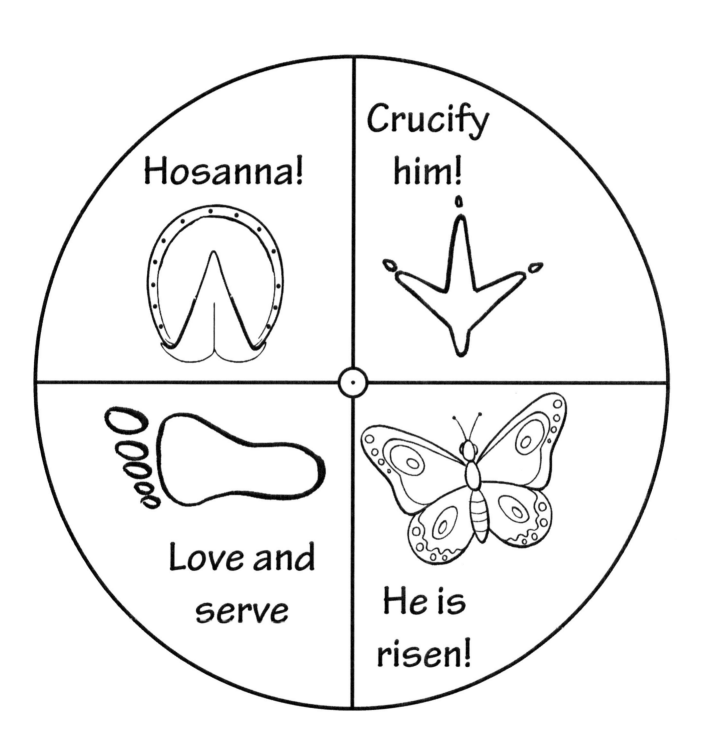

Easter - Workshop 1: Easter footprints
Easter spinner template BOTTOM/BACK

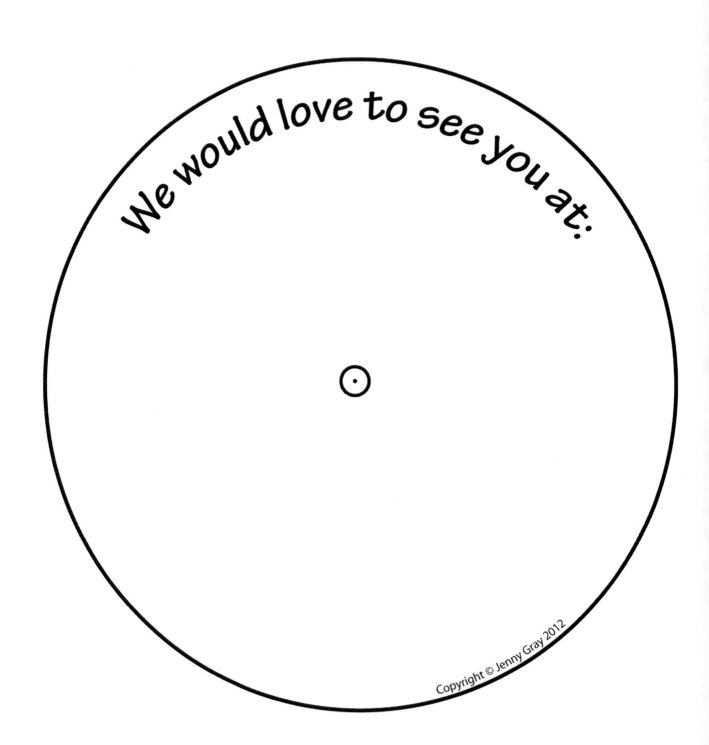

Easter - Workshop 1: Easter footprints
Easter spinner template BOTTOM/BACK

Easter - Workshop 2: Easter words
Easter garden template

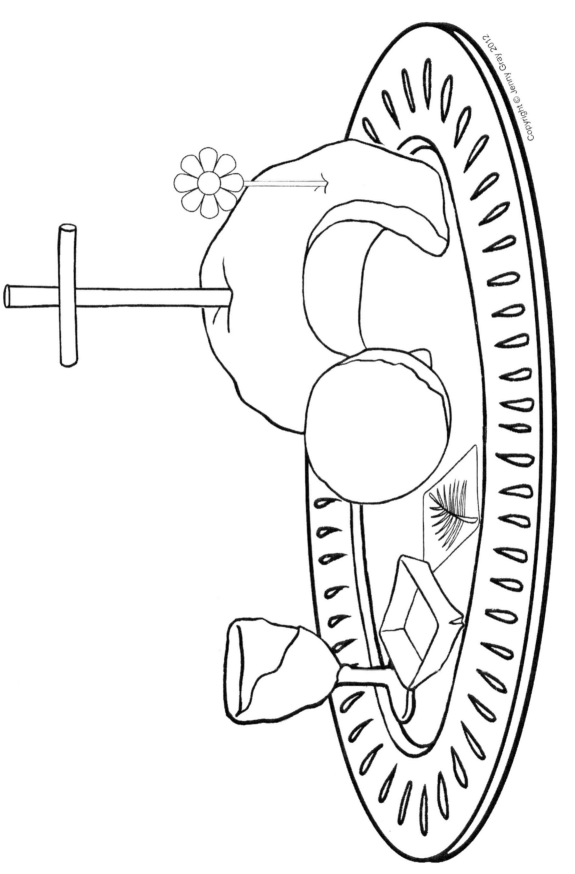

Easter - Workshop 2: Easter words
Invitation template

'Unless a grain of wheat falls into the earth and dies, it remains just a single grain; but if it dies, it bears much fruit.'

John 12.24

We'd love to see you at any of our Easter services or events:

'Unless a grain of wheat falls into the earth and dies, it remains just a single grain; but if it dies, it bears much fruit.'

John 12.24

We'd love to see you at any of our Easter services or events:

Easter – Workshop 3: Easter friends
Hot cross bun card template FRONT

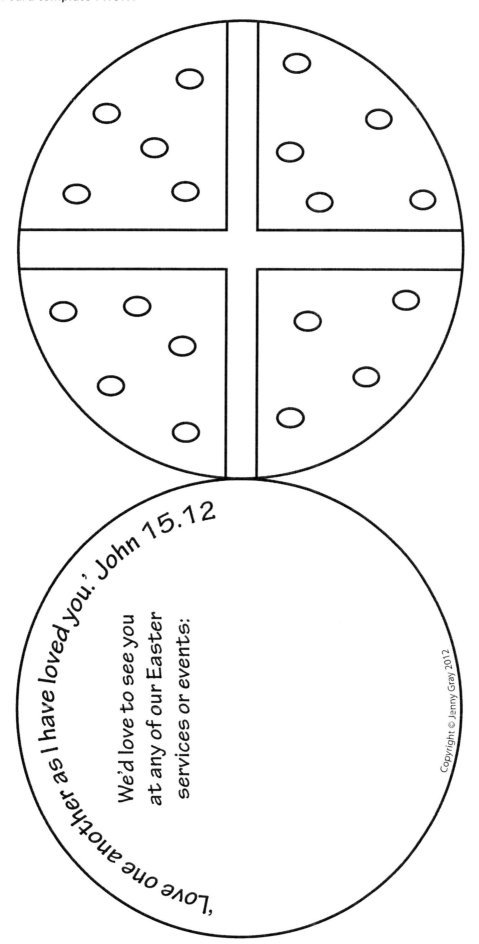

'Love one another as I have loved you.' John 15.12

We'd love to see you at any of our Easter services or events:

Copyright © Jenny Gray 2012

Easter - Workshop 3: Easter friends
Hot cross bun card template BACK

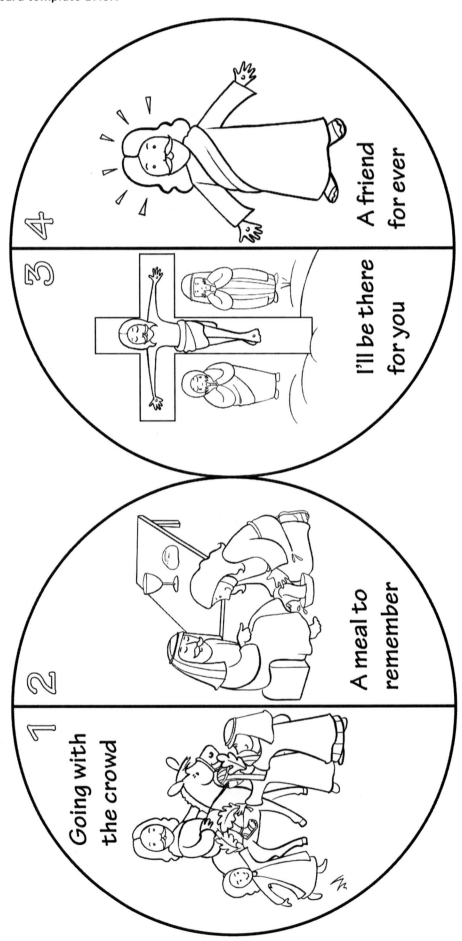

Easter – Workshop 2: Eggy Easter
Easter egg card template FRONT

'No one has greater love than this, to lay down one's life for one's friends.' John 15.13

Easter - Workshop 4: Eggy Easter
Easter egg card template BACK

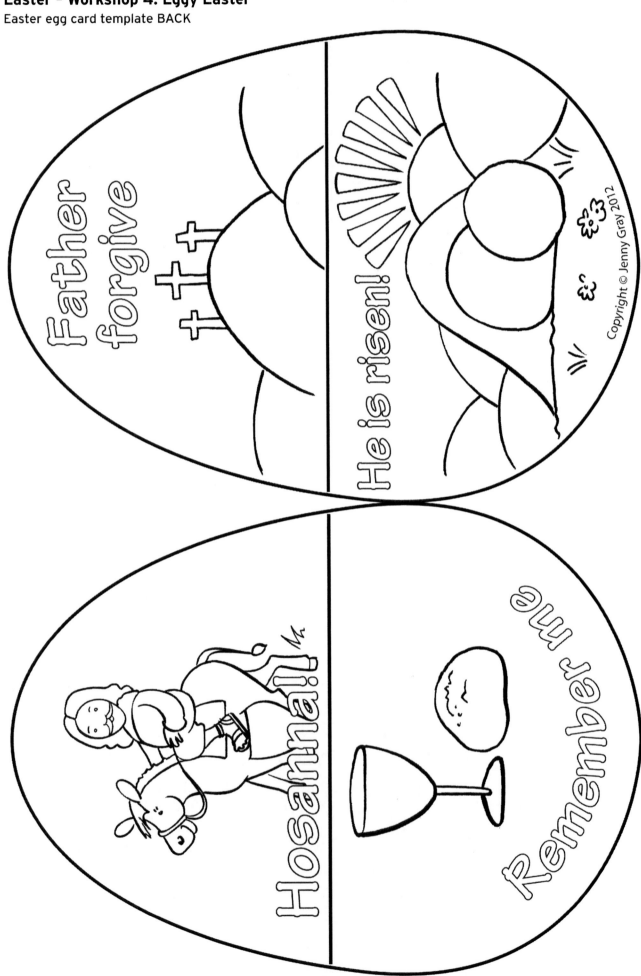

Father forgive

He is risen!

Copyright © Jenny Gray 2012

Hosanna!

Remember me

Jesus – Workshop 1: Jesus' special prayer
Paper game template

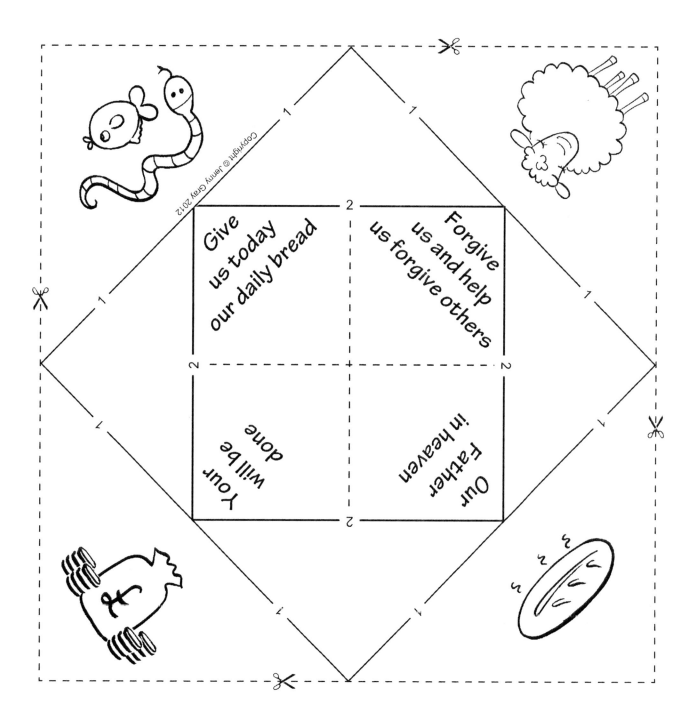

Give us today our daily bread

Forgive us and help us forgive others

Your will be done

Our Father in heaven

Copyright © Jenny Gray 2012

Jesus – Workshop 1: Jesus' special prayer
Invitation template

Our Father in heaven,
hallowed be your name,
your kingdom come,
your will be done,
on earth as in heaven.
Give us today our daily bread,
forgive us our sins
as we forgive those who sin against us.
Lead us not into temptation
but deliver us from evil.
For the kingdom, the power and the glory
are yours, now and for ever. Amen.

We'd love to see you at one of our summer events:

Our Father in heaven,
hallowed be your name,
your kingdom come,
your will be done,
on earth as in heaven.
Give us today our daily bread,
forgive us our sins
as we forgive those who sin against us.
Lead us not into temptation
but deliver us from evil.
For the kingdom, the power and the glory
are yours, now and for ever. Amen.

We'd love to see you at one of our summer events:

Jesus - Workshop 2: Four faces of Jesus
Cross template

Jesus is angry

Jesus cries

Jesus laughs

Jesus loves

'Whoever has seen

me has seen the

Father.'

John 14.9

Jesus - **Workshop 3: Jesus changes lives**
Colour-by-letters template FRONT:
easy - top; harder - bottom

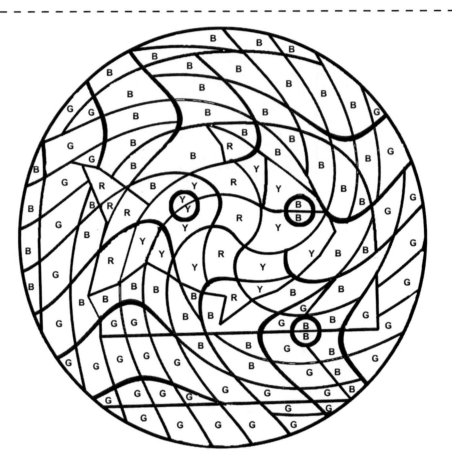

Jesus – Workshop 3: Jesus changes lives
Colour-by-letters (invitation) template BACK

Jesus says:

'I have come so you may have life, in all its fullness.'

John 10.10

We'd love to see you at one of our summer events:

Jesus says:

'I have come so you may have life, in all its fullness.'

John 10.10

We'd love to see you at one of our summer events:

Jesus - Workshop 4: Who is Jesus?
Example of hand template

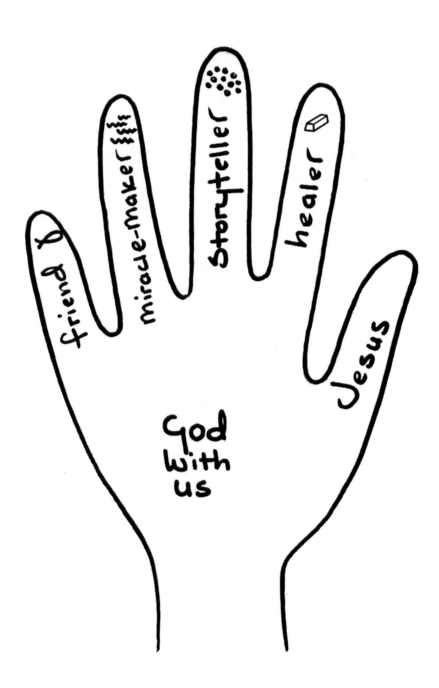

Jesus - Workshop 4: Who is Jesus?
Example of hand template

Jesus – Workshop 4: Who is Jesus?
Invitation template

'No one has ever seen God. It is God the only Son ... who has made him known.'

John 1.18

We'd love to see you at one of our summer events:

'No one has ever seen God. It is God the only Son ... who has made him known.'

John 1.18

We'd love to see you at one of our summer events:

11
Additional resources

Key Stage 1 class visits to your church

This flexible resource is divided into eight activities. Choose which you need, in any order, to fill your time slot and meet the school's requirements. In Hertfordshire (at the time of writing), Year 1 explores belonging to a religious community and baptism, while Year 2 looks at Christian signs and symbols, including the Eucharist or Communion, what Christians do in church, the role and work of a priest or minister or pastor. The topics covered in your local area will probably be similar. This workshop can be run with just a leader and a helper. The parts one to five listed below are intended for the whole class and parts six to eight for small groups.

1 Welcome

2 Church building quiz

3 People in church

4 Holy Communion, the Eucharist, Lord's Supper or Mass

5 Baptism

6 Stained-glass window(s)

7 Look around the church in small groups

8 Outside the church (weather permitting)

The materials you will need are listed at the start of each section below. You will also need a CD player and CDs if you want to play music as the children enter and leave the church (see Engaging the senses, page 22). Drinks and biscuits can be provided as a sign of hospitality, or schools may bring their own.

Welcome

Materials required   Large picture of Jesus welcoming children (Turvey[1] or other).

Leader   **Introduction**

(*Welcome the children at the church door and lead them to the pews or seats at the front of the church. Invite them to put their coats and so on under the pews or seats to be collected at the end of the session.*)

Welcome to our church. Hands up if you have been to a church before . . . if you have been to this church . . .

(*Show the large picture of Jesus welcoming children.*) I wonder who is in the picture . . . It's Jesus with lots of children. Jesus thinks all children are special. Jesus always has time for children, which is why we love to welcome you to our church.

Church building quiz

Materials required 15 laminated labels for different parts of the church (see examples listed below, but as appropriate for your church), Blu-Tack.

Helper Let's begin with a quiz to find out about the church. You can put a label on the special things we find.

1 Special books used in services . . . *(hymn books)*.

2 A large musical instrument used in church . . . *(organ)*.

3 Bench seats for the people, the congregation, to sit on . . . *(pew)*.

4 The path down the middle of the church . . . *(aisle)*.

5 The table at the top of the steps . . . *(altar)*.

6 Special seats for people who sing . . . *(choir stalls)*.

7 A high place to talk from . . . *(pulpit)*.

8 Where the Bible is read . . . *(lectern)*.

9 A special place for children . . . *(children's corner)*.

10 A quiet place to pray and think . . . *(chapel)*.

11 This is used for christenings, baptisms . . . *(font)*.

12 Where the priest/minister gets ready . . . *(vestry)*.

13 A symbol or badge for Christians . . . *(cross)*.

14 A place to remember people who have died . . . *(book of remembrance or gravestones or plaques)*.

15 A place to meet, eat, drink and chat . . . *(hall)*.

Is there anything you want to say or ask . . . ?

I wonder what people do in church . . . There are clues in the things we've just labelled together . . . *(Prompt as needed by going to the different places yourself – for example:*

- *sing hymns, read the Bible, say prayers;*
- *listen to a sermon or talk to learn more about God and Jesus;*
- *come to be baptized or christened or married or for a funeral;*
- *share bread and wine at the altar, called Holy Communion, Mass, the Eucharist, Lord's Supper;*
- *meet with other Christians in the hall;*
- *other.)*

People in church

Materials required Clothes and props to indicate roles in church (see below for suggestions, but as appropriate for your church).

Helper A church isn't just a building – it's the people who follow Jesus. I wonder if you know this little finger rhyme. Watch me, then you can join in too.

Here's the church	*(join hands, fingers interleaved and pointing down)*
here's the steeple	*(point index fingers upwards, meeting at tips)*
look inside and here are the people	*(turn hands upwards and wiggle fingers.)*

We'll see some of the people who make up this church – your teacher can find me some volunteers to come to the front and be dressed up as a:

- priest/minister – alb, stole, chasuble *(show different colours for different seasons)*
- lay reader – cassock, surplice, blue scarf
- member of the choir – cassock, surplice, ruff, medals
- server – alb, holds candle, helps the priest/minister during services.

These people wear uniforms – like you wear a school uniform. Your teacher may like to take some photographs of you dressed up . . . *(See note about photography, page 18.)*

Most people in church, however, just wear their ordinary clothes: *(Invite the other children to come and stand at the front alongside those who are dressed up, with the following props. This should involve the whole class of 30 children, so double up a job if necessary.)*

- verger or caretaker – keys to lock up the church;
- organist or pianist or music group – music book;
- people to read from the Bible – a Bible;
- people to say prayers – prayer list, folder or book;
- people to take the collection – a basket;
- welcomers – leaflets to hand out;
- sound desk – microphone;
- Sunday school team – worksheet;
- crèche – toys;
- coffee team – mug and jar of coffee;
- people who give lifts to church – car keys;
- office staff – newsletter;
- magazine team – magazine;
- cleaning team – brush;
- those who clean and iron the linen on the altar – cloth;
- gardening and maintenance team – fork, paintbrush;
- flower team – watering can;
- treasurer – money bag;
- those who visit the sick at home and in hospital – church card;
- lunch club team – plate, knife and fork;
- toddler group – toys;
- youth clubs – game controller;
- study group leaders – book;
- charities team – Christian Aid envelope;
- other.

Is there anything you want to say or ask . . . ?

Holy Communion, the Eucharist, Lord's Supper or Mass

Materials required Large picture of Jesus at the Last Supper (Turvey or other), small table, cloth, wine bottle, glasses, candles, bread.

Helper *(Show the picture of Jesus at the Last Supper.)* I wonder what's happening in this picture . . . *(Include that Jesus is sharing a meal with his friends on the night before he* *dies. Jesus wants us to share bread and wine to remember him. Christians do this in churches on a Sunday and sometimes on weekdays too.)*

(Set the small table in front of the altar.) Here's my ordinary table. I wonder how I could make it special – for a special meal like a birthday or Christmas or other celebration . . . *(Add cloth, wine bottle, glasses, candles, bread as the children suggest them, prompting, if necessary, by showing them these items.)*

(Point to the altar.) I wonder what you can see here . . . *(Cloth, wine, chalice/cup, candles and special bread.)* Jesus shared the Last Supper with his friends. Christians share bread and wine to remember Jesus and be close to him.

Is there anything you want to say or ask . . . ?

Baptism

Materials required   Large picture of Jesus' baptism (Turvey or other), doll, font or baptism pool, water in a jug, shell, oil, baptismal candle and matches, Bible (or as appropriate for your church).

Helper   *(Move the class near to the font or baptism pool.)* I wonder if anyone has been baptized or christened . . . Some churches baptize grown-ups, but usually babies and young children are baptized.

(Show the picture of Jesus' baptism with John the Baptist.) I wonder what's happening in this picture . . . *(Jesus comes to his cousin John the Baptist to be baptized in the River Jordan. The dove is a sign that God's Holy Spirit is with Jesus. God says, 'This is my beloved son. I am well pleased with him.')* You can see the water and the dove on the baptismal candle . . . *(show).*

Let's go through what happens in this church at a baptism service *(hold doll)*. There are three parts to baptism in this church. The first is to make the sign of the cross with oil *(make sign of the cross with oil on the doll's forehead)*. The cross is a Christian badge, like your school badge – it shows you are part of God's church.

The second part is to pour water over the head in the name of God the Father, Son and Holy Spirit as the child is named *(use the shell or your hand to pour a little water over the doll's head three times)*. Water is a sign of God cleaning us and helping us grow.

In the third part, a lighted candle is given to the family, because Jesus is the 'Light of the world' – he shows us the right way to live *(light the baptismal candle and give it to the teacher)*.

In this church, we give the candle to the family and also give everyone who is baptized a Bible, to help them find out about God and Jesus. I wonder if you have a Bible at home . . . a favourite Bible story . . .

The font is at the back of the church, near the door. I wonder why it is here . . . *(Baptism is the start of being a Christian.)*

Some churches have a big pool that people step into to be baptized. They go right under the water, like you do in a swimming pool. I wonder if you've seen this . . .

Is there anything you want to say or ask . . . ?

Stained-glass window(s)

Materials required Clipboards, paper, pens, wax crayons or felt-tip pens, make template of window for children to colour (optional).

Helper *(Gather near to a stained-glass window.)* I wonder what you can see . . .

I wonder why we have windows like this in church . . . *(Decoration to honour God, teach people the Bible stories, remember a person or event.)*

I wonder what you think about the window(s) . . .

(Give the children clipboards, paper, pens and crayons or felt-tip pens and ask them to draw the whole or part of a window and colour in their drawings, or colour in their copies of the window template.)

Is there anything you want to say or ask . . . ?

Look around the church in small groups

Materials required Clipboards, paper, pens, wax crayons or felt-tip pens, drink and biscuits (optional).

Helper *(In small, supervised groups, the children can explore and experience the church – for example, sit in the choir stalls, climb up into the pulpit, stand at the lectern, sit in a side chapel and children's corner, kneel in the pews or on the kneelers, have a close look at the font and altar, visit any other rooms, such as the vestry, choir room, hall, and dress up and perhaps be photographed by the teacher in robes – see note about photography, page 18.)*

(To engage their senses, the children can:

- *talk about what they see and draw their favourite part of the church;*
- *write or say a prayer, silently or aloud, maybe at a candle stand;*
- *touch wood or stone carvings, brasses, water in the font;*
- *listen to a quiet CD of reflective music, hymns or worship songs;*
- *look for flowers and incense to smell, and you could ask them what the church smells of (polish, musty).)*

Is there anything you want to say or ask . . . ?

Outside the church (weather permitting)

Materials required Clipboards, paper, pens, wax crayons or felt-tip pens.

Helper I wonder how you know from the outside that this building is a church . . .

Is there anything you want to say or ask . . . ?

Adaptations to make for a visit by children with special needs

The materials can be adapted according to the numbers of children and helpers, their special needs and the time allocated for the visit.

The following includes suggestions for small-group activities, a plenary session and refreshments. Five church helpers will be needed to run the small groups and up to five welcomers, who can make refreshments for the children and helpers and assist the small groups.

Welcome

Materials required Large picture of Jesus welcoming children (Turvey[2] or other) near the entrance (but avoid congestion around the porch), drinks and biscuits.

Welcomers *(Children may arrive in small groups, in minibuses, walking or in wheelchairs. Welcomers greet the groups of children and helpers as they arrive, lead them into church.)* Have you been in a/this church before? *(Stop by the large picture of Jesus welcoming children.)*

I wonder who is in the picture . . . *(It's Jesus with lots of children.)* Jesus thinks all children are special. Jesus always has time for children, which is why we love to welcome you to church.

We're going to find out what people do in church. *(Lead the children to the small-group helpers and return to the porch to greet the next group of arrivals. When all the children have arrived, prepare the drinks and lay out the biscuits for the helpers and children to have in the small groups.)*

Group 1: People sing in church

Materials required Choir robes, hymn books, hymn numbers to go on hymn board, musical instruments (as appropriate for your church).

Helper *(Show the children where the members of the choir sit. Invite them to sit or stand in the choir stalls if they are able. Dress the children or helpers in choir robes or lay robes over children in wheelchairs, if they wish. Look at hymn books together – invite them to choose a verse of a favourite hymn or song to sing, with musical instruments chosen from the selection. Locate the organ, piano, drums . . . carefully play any instruments.)*

Is there anything you want to say or ask . . . ?

Group 2: People read the Bible in church

Materials required Bible, lectern, selection of children's Bibles, as appropriate for your church.

Helper *(Show the children where people stand to read the Bible. Invite them to stand at the lectern, if they want to and are able. Show the children the selection of children's Bibles.)* Do you have a Bible at school or at home . . . ? Do you have a favourite Bible story . . . ?

Is there anything you want to say or ask . . . ?

Group 3: People pray in church

Materials required Order of service sheets or book, intercessions book, candle stand, kneelers (as appropriate for your church).

Helper   Prayers are talking to God. We can say 'thank you' for the good things we enjoy, 'sorry' for what we do wrong and 'please', asking God's help for ourselves and people who are sick or sad.

When we pray, we shut our eyes to help us concentrate. Sometimes people kneel . . . *(invite the children to kneel if they want and are able to).*

Sometimes people light a candle . . . *(Light a candle at the candle stand for the group.)*

Do you say prayers . . . ? *(Invite all to close their eyes and thank God for something good – families, friends, pets, teachers, sunshine.)*

(Show the children prayers in the service sheets or book. Invite them to write or dictate a prayer if they wish, maybe just the name of someone to pray for.)

Is there anything you want to say or ask . . . ?

Group 4: People share bread and wine in church

Materials required   Large picture of the Last Supper (Turvey or other), altar, bread, wine, as appropriate for your church.

Helper   *(Show large picture of the Last Supper.)* I wonder what is happening in this picture . . . *(Christians share bread and wine in church to remember Jesus at the Last Supper. Show the children the altar, bread and wine.)*

Do you have bread and wine in church . . . ?

Is there anything you want to say or ask . . . ?

Group 5: People are baptized in church

Materials required   Oil, doll, font or pool, baptismal candle and matches, children's Bible, as appropriate for your church.

Helper   *(Gather the children round the font or pool.)* Baptism is a welcome into God's family. A cross is the special Christian badge – like your school badge. Does anyone have a cross/crucifix . . . ?

Baptism begins with the sign of the cross. *(Make the sign of the cross on the doll's head with the oil.)*

Water is poured over the baby's or child's head – water for cleaning, water for growth . . . *(Pour water over the doll's head.)*

A baptismal candle is given – God's light to guide us . . . *(Light the baptismal candle.)*

Have any of you been baptized . . . ?

Is there anything you want to say or ask . . . ?

(Welcomers give the small groups refreshments and look around the church with them as needed.)

Plenary session

Materials required   Box of musical instruments, CD of worship songs (choose songs they know or sing that have actions, such as 'Jesus' love is very wonderful',[3] 'He's got the whole world in his hands'[4]), as appropriate for your church.

Welcomer   Thank you for coming. We are going to end by singing some songs together to God, and I hope you will join in the actions.

Christmas presentation for nursery and/or reception classes

Note that it is not a legal requirement for children in nursery schools or classes to receive religious education, but the school curriculum must promote children's spiritual, moral, social and cultural development. In Hertfordshire, nursery classes may look at the importance to Christians of giving presents, while reception classes may explore Christmas as Jesus' birthday. The topics covered in your local area will probably be similar.

Adaptations for visits from children with special needs

If this Christmas presentation is offered in a church, the welcomers can greet the groups of children as they arrive and lead them into the church. The children may arrive in small groups, minibuses, walking or in wheelchairs. Christmas carols can be played and instruments handed out as the groups arrive. Drinks and biscuits can be offered before they leave. The presentation can be shortened or simplified as required.

Materials required Nativity set in a wrapped shoebox and glove puppets (optional), large pictures of Mary and the angel Gabriel, Mary, Joseph and a donkey, Jesus in the manger, the shepherds being visited by the angel, the wise men (Turvey[5] or other), gold, frankincense and myrrh, Christmas cracker, CD of Christmas carols that includes 'Little donkey' and 'Away in a manger', plus 'Let's go, let's go', with actions,[6] 'Here we go up to Bethlehem' sung to the tune of 'Here we go round the mulberry bush', with actions, CD player, Christmas cards[7] (optional – find templates or teachers may prefer children to draw their own pictures).

Leader Good morning everyone. It's not long until the Christmas holidays. I wonder what's special about Christmas . . . (The children may say presents, Father Christmas, Christmas trees, it's Jesus' birthday.)

(Show the wrapped shoebox.) I wonder what's inside my present . . . I need someone to help me open it . . . (With the help of a child, bring out the pieces of the Nativity set.)

This will help us find out about Christmas and why we have lovely presents.

The story begins with an angel and a girl. (Give out the Nativity figures of an angel and Mary and the glove puppets, if using, for the children to hold up. Show the picture of Mary and the angel Gabriel and piece the story together as follows.) The angel in the Christmas story is called . . . (Gabriel) and the girl is called . . . (Mary). Angels bring messages from God and, this time, God sends the angel Gabriel to Mary to ask her to be the mother of his Son, a special baby called . . . (Jesus).

I wonder how Mary feels when she sees the angel . . . I wonder how you would feel . . . (Prompt if needed, as follows.) Do you think she is surprised . . . ? Do you think she is scared . . . ? Do you think she is pleased that God has chosen her to be the mother of Jesus . . . ? Mary is surprised and scared, but she knows that we can always trust God, so Mary says 'Yes'.

Next, Mary and Joseph go to Bethlehem. (Give out the Nativity figures of Mary, Joseph and the donkey and the glove puppets, if using, for the children to hold up. Have the large picture of Mary, Joseph and a donkey at the front.) Mary is going to marry Joseph. They live in a village called Nazareth, but they have to go to a town called Bethlehem to register to pay their taxes. It's a long way away. How do you think they travel there . . . ? (By donkey.)

(Listen to the CD of the carol 'Little donkey' or simply sing, with the actions – pat each knee in turn to make clip clop sounds, pretend to ring bells, make a diamond star *shape with hands together, then repeat the clip clop. Alternatively, you could sing another carol.)*

Then, there's no room at the inn. *(Give out the Nativity figures of Mary, Joseph and the innkeeper and glove puppets, if using, for the children to hold up. Show the picture of Jesus in the manger.)* Bethlehem is very busy. Lots of people have come to register to pay their taxes. Where can Mary and Joseph stay . . . ? *(A kind innkeeper lets them stay in his stable.)* That night, baby Jesus is born. There's no bed or cot for baby Jesus, so Mary puts him in the . . . *(Manger, the animals' feeding trough, to sleep.)* I wonder what it's like in a stable . . . Do you think that you would like to sleep in a manger . . . ?

(Listen to the carol 'Away in a manger' on the CD and sing or choose another.)

The next key part of the story is the shepherds coming to visit Jesus. *(Give out the shepherds and angel Nativity figures and the glove puppets, if using, for the children to hold up. Hold up the picture of the shepherds being visited by the angel.)*

The shepherds are looking after their sheep on the hillside. An angel comes to tell them about Jesus, the new baby king. I wonder how the shepherds feel when they see an angel . . . *(Prompt, if needed.)* Do you think they are surprised . . . ? Do you think they are scared . . . ? Do you think they are pleased . . . ?

The shepherds leave their sheep and go to . . . *(Bethlehem, to the stable, to see the special baby. Stand up and sing 'Let's go, let's go' with actions, or another song.)*

Then the wise men come to see Jesus. *(Give out the Nativity figures of the wise men and glove puppets, if using, for the children to hold up. Also, hold up the large picture of the wise men.)* The wise men live far away in the East, but what is it they see . . . ? *(A special star in the sky.)* The star tells them that a new king of the Jews has been born. The wise men follow the star to . . . *(Bethlehem, to the stable, to see the special baby.)* The wise men bring special presents . . . *(Gold, frankincense and myrrh.)* When we give presents at Christmas, we remember the wise men's presents and Jesus, who is God's present to us.

Now let's stand up and sing 'Twinkle, twinkle little star' *(the traditional nursery rhyme, with actions, if known).* Let's sing it again with these words:

> Twinkle, twinkle, little star, how I wonder what you are.
> Up above the world so high – show wise men where Jesus lies,
> Twinkle, twinkle, little star, how I wonder what you are.

The wise men bring their gifts to Jesus. I wonder what gifts we can give him . . . *(Our singing, smiles, thank yous, helping others every day, giving toys to people in need, filling Christingle Candles with coins to help runaway children in need.)*

We have crackers at Christmas *(show the cracker)* – we can pull one now to remind us of the Christmas story:

- the paper crown reminds us that Jesus is a special king;
- the message reminds us of the angels' message to Mary and the shepherds;
- the gift reminds us of the wise men's presents and Jesus, who is God's present to us;
- the bang reminds us of the surprise of Christmas – a baby born in a stable, Jesus, God with us.

Christmas is Jesus' birthday. Shall we stand and sing 'Happy birthday' to Jesus . . . ?

(Happy birthday to you, happy birthday to you. Happy birthday, dear Jesus, happy birthday to you.)

We've now heard about the key moments in the Christmas story – let's remember it with an action song – 'Here we go up to Bethlehem' *(to the tune of 'Here we go round the mulberry bush', with actions)*. We need to stand and move around in a big circle as we sing, 'Here we go up to Bethlehem. We found a stable in Bethlehem . . . *(point hands together to make the stable)* Jesus was born in . . . *(rock arms)*. The star shone over . . . *(make a diamond star shape with both hands)*. The angels sang in . . . *(wave arms up and down to make wings)*. Shepherds came to . . . *(clench fist to hold a staff)*. Kings brought gifts to . . . *(hold hands out in front)'*.

Are there some other songs that you would like to sing . . . ? Is there anything you want to ask or say . . . ?

(The children can then colour a Christmas card or draw their own Christmas pictures. As they draw and colour, they can talk about their favourite part of the Christmas story, about birthdays, Christmas and presents.)

Easter presentation for nursery and/or reception classes

Like the Christmas presentation (page 159), this Easter presentation can be offered in church if it is near the school, or in the school if the church is too far for the children to walk.

Adaptations for visits from children with special needs

If this Easter presentation is offered in a church, the welcomers can greet the groups of children as they arrive and lead them into the church. The children may arrive in small groups, minibuses, walking or in wheelchairs. Easter songs can be played and instruments handed out as the groups arrive. Drinks and biscuits can be offered before they leave. The presentation can be shortened or simplified as required.

Materials required   Large pictures of Palm Sunday, the Last Supper and the washing of the feet and the risen Jesus (Turvey[8] or other), palm branches (made of green paper or real), a coconut, halved and cleaned, knitted or other Easter figures, a cross, hot cross buns, Easter egg, box of eggs, Easter cards, flower bulbs, picture of butterfly cocoons, CD or words and music of 'We have a king who rides a donkey',[9] 'Jesus' hands were kind hands',[10] 'Lord, I lift your name on high',[11] 'Jesus is a friend of mine',[12] 'Jesus' love is very wonderful'[13] (how many songs are used is optional), CD player, Easter card to colour (optional – teachers may prefer children to draw their own pictures), paper, crayons and felt-tips.

Leader   Good morning, everyone. It's not long until the Easter holidays. I wonder what's special about Easter . . . *(The children may say Easter eggs – show Easter egg.)*

I've come to help you find out about Easter and why we have these special Easter eggs.

The story begins with Palm Sunday. *(Show the large picture of Palm Sunday, with Jesus on a donkey, and set out the figures of the donkey, Jesus and the crowd with palms.)* I wonder who this is riding into Jerusalem on a donkey . . . *(Jesus).* Crowds of people are cheering Jesus and shouting, 'Hosanna, Hosanna, hurray for Jesus the king!' I wonder if we can be the crowd today and shout, 'Hosanna, hosanna, hurray for Jesus the king!'. Ready, all together, 'Hosanna, Hosanna, hurray for Jesus the king!' . . . Louder, one more time . . .

I know a song about Palm Sunday, which we'll sing to the tune of 'What shall we do with the drunken sailor'. It's 'We have a king who rides a donkey'. If you know it, you can hum the tune with me, then join in.

Crowds often wave flags when they cheer, but this crowd doesn't have flags – they wave branches from palm trees by the road *(hand out the palm branches).* Let's stand up and sing our song again, but this time we'll wave our branches too . . .

(Clap coconut halves together.) I wonder what this noise reminds you of . . . *(The donkey Jesus rides on Palm Sunday.)* Let's clap our hands together to be the donkey too . . .

Do you know that donkeys have a cross on their back? Have a look next time you see a donkey. People say it's because a donkey carries Jesus on Palm Sunday, on his way to the cross on Good Friday.

Now it's Thursday, Maundy Thursday. *(Show the large pictures of Jesus at the Last Supper with his friends, washing their feet and sharing bread and wine. Set out the figures of Jesus and his friends around the table.)* This is Jesus having a special meal with his friends on the night before he dies. It's called the Last Supper. I wonder what Jesus is doing in these pictures . . . *(He's washing his friends' feet, giving us an example of looking after other people, and sharing a special meal with bread and wine to help his friends remember him.)*

(Show coconut halves.) This is like the bowl of water Jesus uses to wash his friends' feet. This is like the cup of wine to help his friends remember him. Christians eat bread and drink wine in church to remember Jesus. See if you can cup your hands to make the bowl and the cup too . . .

Jesus uses his hands to do kind things, like wash his friends' feet and share bread and wine. I wonder if we can do kind things with our hands too . . . *(Maybe we can help people, share our toys, care for our families and friends and pets.)*

Let's look at our hands now and listen to a song, 'Jesus' hands were kind hands'. I'll say each line, then you can repeat it after me and do the actions, like me.

> kind hands *(one hand strokes the other).*
> blessing *(hold hand out in blessing).*
> My hands *(hold hands out in front).*
> kind hands *(one hand strokes the other).*

Now it's Friday, Good Friday. *(Show the cross and a hot cross bun.)* This is a sad day. The crowds turn against Jesus. Jesus dies on the cross on a hill outside the city of Jerusalem. *(Turn a coconut half over to be the hill and show the three marks – they are like the marks of the three crosses on the hill, three because two other people died with Jesus.)* Try turning one of your hands over and making it into a hill too . . . We'll pretend three of our knuckles are the marks of the three crosses . . .

We have hot cross buns at Easter to remember Jesus dying on the cross on Good Friday. *(If the teacher agrees, break up a bun and give the children a bit to taste if they want to.)*

Good Friday is sad, but it's not the end of the story. Jesus' friends take him down from the cross and put him in a tomb – a cave in the rock. They roll a stone to close it up. *(Show one coconut half.)* This is the cave and the other half of the coconut is the stone to cover it. Try making one hand into the tomb *(cup it with the hand on its side)* and the other hand can be the stone to go in front . . .

Now it's Sunday, Easter Day. *(Show the large picture of the risen Jesus. Set out the figures of Jesus and Mary by the open (coconut) tomb.)* This is Jesus on Easter Day. The stone's been rolled away, the tomb is empty *(show the open empty coconut half)*. Jesus' friends meet Jesus again. It's a big surprise, but they're so happy Jesus is alive. Let's take one hand away from our hand tombs – that's the stone rolled away. Look inside your hand tomb . . . It's empty because Jesus is alive . . .

We have chocolate eggs at Easter to celebrate that Jesus is alive. The shell of the egg is like the empty tomb *(unwrap Easter egg and show)*.

We send Easter cards *(show)* with pictures of new life . . . little baby chicks, spring flowers, butterflies, lambs and rabbits. Baby chicks come out of dead-looking eggs *(show)*, flowers come out of dead-looking bulbs *(show)*, butterflies come out of dead-looking cocoons *(show)*, like Jesus comes out of the tomb.

Let's go through the Easter story again, using the pictures, the coconut and our hands. You can fill in the blanks for me.

We begin with . . . *(Palm Sunday – the teacher can hold up the picture, you clap the coconut halves, the children clap their hands.)* This is . . . *(Jesus riding into Jerusalem on a donkey).*

Now it's . . . *(Maundy Thursday - the teacher can hold up the pictures, you hold out a coconut half as a bowl, the children cup their hands into a bowl.)* This is Jesus washing his friends' feet, this is Jesus sharing bread and wine with his friends.

Now it's . . . *(Good Friday - the teacher can hold up the cross and hot cross bun, you use a coconut half as a hill, the children make a hand into a hill.)* Jesus dies on the . . . *(cross)*. Then Jesus is buried in the tomb with a stone to close it *(use hands to make tomb and stone)*.

At last it's . . . *(Easter Day - the teacher can hold up the picture, you open the coconut tomb, the children open their hands and look inside.)* The stone has been rolled away. Look inside your hand tomb. It's empty because Jesus is alive.

(Optional.) Let's end with some songs about Jesus to remember Easter. You can stand up and copy me. *(Sing along to the CD of 'Lord, I lift your name on high', 'Jesus is a friend of mine' and others, as you decide.)*

We can't see Jesus now, but he is with us all the time. Jesus loves us and helps us look after each other and after God's world. *(Sing 'Jesus' love is very wonderful' with actions.)*

So high *(stretch up)*
so low *(bend down)*
so wide *(reach out)*.
love *(place both hands on heart)*.

Are there other songs that you would like to sing? Is there anything you want to ask?

(The children can colour an Easter card or draw their own Easter pictures. As they draw and colour, they can talk about their favourite part of the Easter story, Easter eggs, egg hunts and other Easter activities.)

Notes

Introduction: What is RE Active Church?

1 Lucy Moore, *Messy Church* and *Messy Church 2* (Abingdon, BRF, 2006).

2 Vincent J. Donovan, in *Christianity Rediscovered* (London, SCM Press, 2001), understands evangelism as helping people recognize the God who is present in everyone and all of life.

3 Lucinda Neall, at <www.aboutourboys.com>

4 Rebecca Nye, *Children's Spirituality* (London, Church House Publishing, 2009), page 88.

5 Nye, page 89.

1 Working with schools

1 Visit <www.whychurch.org.uk>

2 Figures quoted from Peter Brierley, *Reaching and Keeping Tweenagers* (Swindon, Christian Research, 2003), page 133.

3 The Revd Lynda Barley, former Church of England Head of Research and Statistics: 'some encouraging signs such as numbers of under 16s in church holding steady and growth in church attendance in 16 of 44 dioceses', Church of England's website, Media Centre section, under 'Top news releases' at: <www.churchofengland.org/media-centre/news/2011/02/provisional-attendance-figures-for-2009-released-attending-a-local-cofe-church-continues-to-be-part-of-a-typical-week-for-11-million-people.aspx>

4 Mike Chew and Mark Ireland, *How to do Mission Action Planning* (London, SPCK, 2009).

5 Point 11, GS 1835B, 'Mission Action Planning in the Church of England: A briefing note from the Mission and Public Affairs Council', Mission and Public Affairs Council (June 2011).

6 Quoted in *Church Times*, 22 July 2011.

7 Figures quoted from Brierley, page 111.

8 Brierley, page 111.

9 Brierley, page 105.

10 Echoed by Margaret Withers, *Where are the Children?* (Abingdon, BRF, 2005).

11 Paul Haynes and Jane Earl, *The Story of RE Inspired by David Skinner* (Abingdon, BRF, 2011).

12 Stream, Sacred Spaces in Schools (172 High Street, London SE20 7QS, tel: 020 8778 3181, email: <admin@streamwork.org.uk>).

13 Diocese of Gloucester resources, Experience Festivals series by Jumping Fish, Diocese of Gloucester Resource Centre, 9 College Green, Gloucester GL1 2LX, tel: 01452 835560, email: <jumpingfish@glosdioc.org.uk>

14 Slough Baptist Church's presentations to Year 6 pupils, Christmas Unwrapped and Easter Cracked, at: <www.sloughbaptistchurch.org.uk/schoolsweek>

15 Reg Bailey, 'Letting children be children: Report of an independent review of the commercialisation and sexualisation of childhood' (Department for Education, June 2011). Also available online at: <www.education.gov.uk/publications/standard/publicationDetail/Page1/CM%208078>

16 Professor Tanya Byron, 'Safer children in a digital world: The report of the Byron Review' (DCSF, 2008). Also available online at: <http://media.education.gov.uk/assets/files/pdf/s/safer%20children%20in%20a%20digital%20world%20the%202008%20byron%20review.pdf>

17 Professor David Buckingham, 'The impact of the commercial world on children's wellbeing: Report of an independent assessment' (DCSF, 2009). Also available online at: <www.education.gov.uk/publications/eOrderingDownload/00669-2009DOM-EN.pdf>

18 Dr Linda Papadopoulos, 'Sexualisation of young people review' (Home Office, 26 February 2010). Also available online at: <www.wrc.org.uk/includes/documents/cm_docs/2010/s/sexualisationyoungpeople.pdf>

19 Visit <www.whychurch.org.uk>

20 A prayer card can be sent to schools to tell them they are being prayed for and ask for particular prayer needs.

21 Figures quoted in Brierley, page 192.

22 Brierley, page 135.

23 St Albans and Harpenden area's Christian Education Project (Step) at: <www.stepschoolswork.org.uk>

3 Getting RE Active Church started

1 Guides for house group leaders are useful for leading any small group. There are many new guides on the Internet and older material, such as CPAS' 'A handbook for house group leaders' (1988) and Patsy Kettle's *What? Me a house group leader?* (Grove Pastoral Series 18, 1984). Some dioceses produce their own material, such as the Diocese of St Albans' 'Working with small groups' (2004).

2 To make your own soft modelling dough, you need 2 teaspoons cream of tartar, 1 cup plain flour, $\frac{1}{2}$ cup salt, 1 tablespoon oil, 1 cup water, food colouring to make it the colour needed. Put all the ingredients into a saucepan over a gentle heat. Mix to a smooth paste and continue to heat gently, stirring continuously until the dough comes away from the sides of the pan, forming a ball. It will be hard to stir at the end. Take the pan off the heat and, when the dough is cool enough to handle, knead it for a few minutes. Put the pan to soak in cold water immediately. Keep the dough in a plastic bag in an airtight container in the fridge or a cool place.

4 RE Active Church resources: Essential elements

1 American educationalist Edgar Dale's 'Cone of Experience' diagram (1946).

2 The Benedictine Nuns of Turvey Abbey's series of posters from McCrimmons at: <www.mccrimmons.com>

3 Sieger Köder series of posters available online at: <www.pauline-uk.org>

4 On the Internet, search using the phrases 'pictures of Jesus laughing' or 'The Christ We Share' for pictures produced by CMS/USPG (2004), available at: <www.cms-uk.org>

5 Otto Huber and Christian Stuckl, *Passion Play 2010 Oberammergau* (London, Prestel, 2010).

6 See <www.tvlicensing.co.uk>

7 Visit: <www.thebricktestament.com> The creator of this site does require permission to use his materials. For information about how to obtain permission, go to <www.thebricktestament.com/churches/index.html>

5 Christmas

1 Search on YouTube for 'Super Duper Christmas' song, by Maranatha! Music.

2 'Just being together', lyrics and music by Andrew Oxspring, Edgy Productions (2008).

3 Sydney Carter, 'Here we go up to Bethlehem', copyright © 1965 Stainer & Bell Ltd. Visit: <www.stainer.co.uk/hymns/advent>

4 Traditional Caribbean.

5 Free archive of optical illusions is available at: <www.123opticalillusions.com>

6 See note 5, above.

7 Use 'The Christ We Share' pictures produced by CMS/USPG (2004), available at: <www.cms-uk.org>, or search the Internet for free pictures.

8 The Benedictine Nuns of Turvey Abbey's 'Jesus Our Light' series of posters from McCrimmons at: <www.mccrimmons.com> or search the Internet for free pictures.

9 The idea came from a *Church Times* cover, but you could make your own using the words and any picture of Jesus.

10 Some schools have filled shoeboxes for our church.

11 Visit: <www.crisis.org.uk>

12 The Children's Society, 'Make runaways safe: Launch report' (July 2011). Also available online at: <www.childrenssociety.org.uk/sites/default/files/tcs/make_runaways_safe_report.pdf>

6 Easter

1 You can download free religious images – search using the phrase 'images for Palm Sunday', for example.

2 The Benedictine Nuns of Turvey Abbey's 'Jesus Our Way' series of posters from McCrimmons at: <www.mccrimmons.com>; Sieger Köder series of posters available online at: <www.pauline-uk.org>; or search the Internet for free pictures.

3 See note 2 for Chapter 3, above.

4 See <www.outoftheark.co.uk>

5 Download music from YouTube, an MP3, search for the lyrics to the *Friends* theme tune or buy a CD.

6 Mark and Helen Johnson, 'He'll Be There', *Songs for EVERY Assembly* (Hampton, Out of the Ark Music, 1999).

7 Paul Mazak, 'Jesus is a friend of mine', copyright © 1974 Celebration/ThankyouMusic.

8 The Benedictine Nuns of Turvey Abbey's 'Jesus Our Way' series of posters from McCrimmons at: <www.mccrimmons.com> or search the Internet for free pictures.

9 Buy two pieces of trellis (each 1.5 or 1.8m/5 or 6 feet long), cut a third off one, then lay the longer piece remaining across the intact piece of trellis and attach them firmly to each other with wire or string to make a simple cross.

10 Rick Founds, 'Lord, I lift your name on high', copyright © 1989 Maranatha! Music/CopyCare.

11 Neil Thorogood and Robert Harvey, *A Road to the Garden* (London, URC, 2005) or search the Internet for free pictures.

12 To make an Easter tree, arrange bare branches in a vase and decorate with little eggs, chicks, butterflies, flowers and so on.

13 Founds, 'Lord, I lift'.

7 Jesus

1 James E. Sneddon, 'Father God in heaven', copyright © 1982 Jubilate Hymns Ltd.

2 See note 2 for Chapter 3, above.

3 For example, Nick Butterworth and Mick Inkpen, *Stories Jesus Told* (Oxford, Candle Books, 2005).

4 The Benedictine Nuns of Turvey Abbey's 'Jesus Our Hope' series of posters from McCrimmons at: <www.mccrimmons.com> or search the Internet for free pictures.

5 Visit: <www.thebricktestament.com> The creator of this site does require permission to use his materials. For information about how to obtain permission, go to <www.thebricktestament.com/churches/index.html>

6 Jo and Nigel Hemming, 'Our God is a great big God', copyright © 2001 Vineyard Songs.

7 Stick the faces of celebrities cut out from magazines on to paper plates. You can then attach a thin garden cane so you can hold the plate up over your face, like a mask, but this is optional. Alternatively, buy ready-made masks.

8 The Benedictine Nuns of Turvey Abbey's 'Jesus Our Hope' series of posters from McCrimmons at: <www.mccrimmons.com> or search the Internet for free pictures.

9 See note 4 for Chapter 4, above.

10 A small poster can be ordered from <www.pauline-uk.org> or you can search the Internet for free pictures.

11 Jeffrey John, *The Meaning in the Miracles* (London, Canterbury Press, 2001) is full of insights.

12 Mark and Helen Johnson, *Songs for EVERY Easter* (Hampton, Out of the Ark Music, 1996), song 'Hosanna'.

13 EMI International Publishing (1970).

14 Paul Mazak (1975), Celebration/ThankyouMusic.

15 The poster can be downloaded from <www.churchads.org.uk/past/1999/index.html>

16 The Benedictine Nuns of Turvey Abbey's 'Jesus Our Hope' series of posters from McCrimmons at: <www.mccrimmons.com> or search the Internet for free pictures.

17 See note 8 for Chapter 6, above.

18 See note 10, above.

19 Gene MacLellan, 'Put your hand in the hand of the man who stilled the waters', copyright © 1970 EMI International Publishing.

20 The Benedictine Nuns of Turvey Abbey's 'Jesus Our Hope' series of posters from McCrimmons at: <www.mccrimmons.com> or search the Internet for free pictures.

21 A 'crown of thorns' can be made from dead honeysuckle or clematis stems, so looks prickly, but won't hurt the children.

11 Additional resources

1 The Benedictine Nuns of Turvey Abbey's 'Jesus Our Hope' series of posters from McCrimmons at: <www.mccrimmons.com>; Sieger Köder series of posters available online at: <www.pauline-uk.org>; or search the Internet for free pictures.

2 The Benedictine Nuns of Turvey Abbey's 'Jesus Our Hope' series of posters from McCrimmons at: <www.mccrimmons.com> or search the Internet for free pictures.

3 'Jesus' love is very wonderful', lyrics by H. W. Rattle, copyright © Scripture Union.

4 D. J. Crawshaw, 'He's got the whole world in His hands', copyright © HarperCollins*Religious*/CopyCare.

5 The Benedictine Nuns of Turvey Abbey's 'Jesus Our Light' series of posters from McCrimmons at: <www.mccrimmons.com> or search the Internet for free pictures.

6 Search on the Internet using the phrase 'children's Christmas songs shepherds' and you will find music, words and actions that you can download.

7 There are lots of religious Christmas pictures to colour on the Internet. For example, visit: <www.squidoo.com/christmascoloring>

8 The Benedictine Nuns of Turvey Abbey's 'Jesus Our Way' series of posters from McCrimmons at: <www.mccrimmons.com> or search the Internet for free pictures.

9 Adapted from lyrics by Fred Kaan, *Junior Praise* (London, Stainer & Bell Ltd), 264. Copyright © 1968 Stainer & Bell Ltd.

10 A. Hopkinson (adapted).

11 Rick Founds, 'Lord, I lift your name on high', copyright © 1989 Maranatha! Music/CopyCare.

12 Founds, 'Lord, I lift'.

13 'Jesus' love is very wonderful', lyrics by H. W. Rattle, copyright © Scripture Union.